# A Crash Course in the Theology of the Body

Naked without Shame (Gen 2:25)

*Second Edition*

## STUDY GUIDE

by Christopher West

# Table of Contents

# About Christopher West

Christopher West is a graduate of the John Paul II Institute for Studies o
Marriage and Family and a visiting professor at the Institute's Melbourn
Australia campus. Formerly the Director of the Office of Marriage an
Family Life for the Archdiocese of Denver, he continues to serve Archbisho
Chaput as an instructor in marriage preparation and deaconate formation, an
as a professor of sexual ethics at St. John Vianney Seminary. He is also th
Theology of the Body Staff Advisor for The GIFT Foundation.

Christopher West's extensive lecturing has taken him to four continents an
his tapes have been distributed around the globe. His first book, *Good New
about Sex and Marriage* is a Catholic best seller and his second book, *Th
Gospel of the Body* will be published in 2003. He resides near Denve
Colorado with his wife and their two sons.

# About The GIFT Foundation

The GIFT Foundation is a not-for-profit, lay Catholic apostolate dedicated t
promoting the Church's teachings on marriage and sexuality. We encourag
men and women, created male and female in the image of God, to make o
their lives a sincere *gift of self*. In this way not only do they discover th
meaning of their lives, but as husband and wife they participate in the ver
mystery of God, Who is Gift. Key components of this mission include edu
cating Catholics on Pope John Paul II's *theology of the body* and on th
important role of Natural Family Planning in living an authentically Christia
marriage.

For more information on The GIFT Foundation (including how to place a
order for tapes, CDs or other products at our low *at-cost* pricing), or to mak
a donation to our mission, please write, call e-mail or visit us online:

**The GIFT Foundation**
P.O. Box 95
Carpentersville, IL 60110
**Tel:** 847-844-1167
**Fax:** 847-844-1195
**E-mail:** info@giftfoundation.org
**Online:** www.giftfoundation.org

# About Naked without Shame
# Second Edition

1999, The GIFT Foundation recorded the first edition of this seminar series nder the title *Naked without Shame: Sex and the Christian Mystery*. In the ears since that first edition, Christopher West has continued to share John aul II's theology of the body with audiences throughout the world. His pres- ntation has gotten better and better.

*A Crash Course in the Theology of the Body (Naked without Shame, econd Edition)*, Christopher West presents John Paul II's vision of marriage nd sexuality with the benefit of these years of experience and growth. icher analogies and more effective, time-tested illustrations bring John aul's insights more clearly to life. Important contexts, qualifications and uances clarify the most difficult and easily misunderstood dimensions of the eology of the body.

nriched by deeper study and wider experience, Christopher West's vibrant resentation has even wider appeal than before, making this second edition of *aked without Shame* the definitive "crash course" in John Paul II's theology f the body.

# About This Study Guide

This Study Guide for *A Crash Course in the Theology of the Body (Naked without Shame, Second Edition)* is offered as a supplement for those who wish to make a more rigorous study of the series. Ample margins are provided for any notes you may wish to take on the series as you go through it with the Study Guide.

## Getting Copies of the Study Guide

Additional bound copies may be purchased from The GIFT Foundation. Like all our products, the Study Guide is offered at the lowest price possible, reflecting only our actual costs.

## Guidelines for Group Study

The Study Guide is especially helpful for group study of the series. Suggestions on conducting a group study of *A Crash Course in the Theology of the Body* are offered in an appendix at the end of the Study Guide.

# A Note on Citations

For ease of reference, all texts from John Paul's catechesis on the body are cited with the page number of the one-volume edition, *The Theology of the Body: Human Love in the Divine Plan* (Pauline Books and Media, 1997). Please note, however, that texts quoted in this study guide are actually taken from the Vatican's original English translation. The one-volume edition published by Pauline was copy-edited and may differ slightly.

Unless otherwise indicated, all cited quotations and paraphrases refer to this one-volume edition of the theology of the body lectures. Other sources are indicated as such by the abbreviations in parentheses.

## Abbreviations

CCC *Catechism of the Catholic Church*

CTH *Crossing the Threshold of Hope*, John Paul II

DV *Dominum et Vivificantem*, John Paul II's encyclical letter on the Holy Spirit

EM *Ecclesia in America*, John Paul II's apostolic exhortation on the Church in America

EV *Evangelium Vitae*, John Paul II's encyclical letter on the Gospel of Life

FC *Familiaris Consortio*, John Paul II's apostolic exhortation on the Role of the Christian Family in the Modern World

FR *Fides et Ratio*, John Paul II's encyclical letter on Faith and Reason

GS *Gaudium et Spes*, Vatican II's Pastoral Constitution on the Church in the Modern World

HV *Humanae Vitae*, Paul VI's encyclical letter concerning the regulation of births

LF *Letter to Families*, John Paul II's Letter to Families in the Year of the Family (1994)

LR *Love and Responsibility*, Karol Wojtyla's philosophical work on human sexuality

MD *Mulieris Dignitatem*, John Paul II's apostolic letter on the Dignity and Vocation of Women

NMI *Novo Millennio Ineunte*, John Paul II's apostolic letter at the close of the Jubilee Year 2000

OL *Orientale Lumen*, John Paul II's apostolic letter on the Light of the East

PC *Person and Community: Selected Essays*, Karol Wojtyla's (trans. Theresa Sandok)

RC *Redemptoris Custos*, John Paul II's apostolic exhortation on Saint Joseph

RH *Redemptor Hominis*, John Paul II's encyclical letter on the Redeemer of Man

RM *Redemptoris Missio*, John Paul II's encyclical letter on the Mission of the Redeemer

SE *Springtime of Evangelization*: John Paul II's 1998 *ad limina* addresses to the Bishops of the United States

SC *Sign of Contradiction*, Karol Wojtyla's Lenten retreat preached to the Roman curia in 1976

TB *The Theology of the Body*, the collection of John Paul II's general audience addresses on Human Love in the Divine Plan

VS *Veritatis Splendor*, John Paul II's Encyclical Letter on the Splendor of Truth

WH *Witness to Hope*, George Weigel's biography of Pope John Paul II

# Preface

Popularizing the Pope's theology of the body is virtually uncharted territory. Although I've been at it for almost ten years, finding the best language, images, and anecdotes remains a process of trial and error. If the past is any indication of the future, I'm sure I could deliver a better series of lectures a few years from now. This is simply my best effort at this stage of my career.

By design, and by necessity of my own limitations, these lectures are not the work of a stellar, academic theologian. Rather, they're the work of a teacher and a catechist trained in theology with an ardent desire to extend the liberating message of the theology of the body beyond the realms of academia. Scholars will forgive me, I hope, if I'm not always as rigorous as they might be in my exposition of the Pope's thought. At the same time, those not trained in theology will forgive me, I hope, if at any point I fail to bring John Paul's theologically dense teaching down to their level.

Theological developments always afford a creative tension in the Church as scholars, catechists, and laymen alike seek to understand them and unfold them. Differences in interpretation and the debates they engender are a healthy part of this process. I, like every interpreter of the Pope's thought, bring my own personal perspectives, gifts, and shortcomings to the table. Hold fast to all that is good and worthy in my efforts, for we can be confident that this good is the Holy Spirit at work despite my imperfections. Leave the rest behind, for that is wholly mine.

Finally, while I can't claim infallibility in my reflections, I can offer the following assurance. All that I present in these lectures is based on my new book, *Theology of the Body Explained: A Commentary on John Paul II's "Gospel of the Body"*, which has been thoroughly reviewed and endorsed by Monsignor Lorenzo Albacete, a mentor and former professor of mine who is a widely recognized expert on John Paul II's theology I refer you to this book for the fullest and most carefully articulated exposition of my thought. And, of course, I also encourage all inclined to do so (especially those with differing perspectives) to measure all of my reflections against the actual text of the Pope.

Christopher West
August 2002

# Suggested Prayers

Prayer is an essential aid in understanding and living John Paul's theology of the body. The prayers below are referenced at various points in the seminar series and may also prove helpful in your own study of the theology of the body and efforts to integrate it into your life.

## 1. Prayer of the "Nuptial Mystery" (I)

"The Spirit and the Bride say, 'Come'" (Rv 22:17). Come, Lord Jesus, open our minds and our hearts to the "great mystery" hidden in the depths of God from all eternity (see Eph 3:9). Give us the eyes to see an image of this "great mystery" in our *creation* as male and female and in our call to become "one body" in marital communion (see Gn 2:24). Give us the eyes to see the definitive revelation of this "great mystery" in our *redemption* as male and female and in our call to become "one body" with you in Eucharistic Communion (see Eph 5:31-32). Plant deep within our breast an abiding hope in the *resurrection of our bodies*, when all who respond to the wedding invitation (see Mt 22:1-14) will behold you face to face, and know you in the eternal consummation of the "Marriage of the Lamb" (see Rv 19:7).

## 2. Prayer of the "Nuptial Mystery" (II)

(This can be repeated as desired or prayed using rosary beads. The first two lines are suggested at the beginning of each decade, the following two lines for each bead of the decade, and the final line at the end of each decade.)

**Bridegroom:** I have loved you with an everlasting love (Jer 31:3). I have betrothed you to me forever (see Hos 2:19). For this reason a man will leave his father and his mother, cling to his bride and the two shall become one flesh (Gn 2:24).

**Bride:** This is a profound mystery, and it refers to Christ and the Church (Eph 5:32).

**Bridegroom:** This is my body given up for you (Lk 22:19).

**Bride:** I believe, I receive, and I give up my body for you.

**Together:** It is consummated (Jn 19:30) and life has been granted to the full (Jn 10:10).

## 3. Prayer for the Redemption of Our Bodies

Come Holy Spirit of truth. Give us the eyes to see the mystery of God revealed through our bodies. Give us the grace to confront the lies we have believed, the lies that have lodged in our hearts that make it so difficult for us to love, accept, and understand our bodies as you created them to be. Dislodge these lies from our hearts that we might behold the body of Christ without shame. For therein – in Christ's exposed body given up for us – the truth is told and Satan's lies defeated. Therein we discover the redemption of our own bodies. Let it be, Lord, according to your Word. Amen.

## 4. Prayer for the Redemption of Sexual Desire

Lord, I praise you and thank you for the gift of my sexual desires. I give all the lustful desires of my heart to you and ask you to crucify them. Grant me the grace and courage to die with you so that I might also be raised with you. By the power of your death and resurrection, untwist in me what sin has twisted so that I might know and experience sexual desire as you created it to be — as the desire to love freely, totally, faithfully, and fruitfully. Amen.

## 5. Prayer in a Moment of Temptation To Lust

You are a woman [man] made in God's image and likeness, never to be looked upon as an object for my gratification. Lord Jesus, grant me the purity of heart to see the image of your glory in the beauty of this woman [man], and order my sexual desires toward true, selfless love. I renounce any tendency within me to use this person for my own selfish pleasure, and I unite all of my sufferings with yours on the cross. Amen.

# INTRODUCTION
# The Human Body, Catholicism and John Paul II

"God speaks to man through the visible creation" (CCC, n. 1147). "The beauty of creation reflects the infinite beauty of the Creator" (CCC, n. 341).

## 1. Epiphany of the Body

According to John Paul, the human body has a "language" that proclaims the mystery of God. This is why he speaks of the body as a *theology*. Yet, because of sin, our vision is blurred. We are in need of an epiphany if we are to "read" the language of the body correctly.

- The body is a "temple of the Holy Spirit" (1 Co 6:19).
- In the mystery of its masculine and feminine beauty and the "one flesh," union the body proclaims the "great mystery" of Christ and the Church (see Eph 5:31-32).
- Because of sin, we are dyslexic and sometimes even illiterate when it comes to reading this theological "language" of the body
- John Paul's theology of the body is like a pair of reading glasses that brings the Word proclaimed by the body into focus.

## 2. Nakedness without Shame

In our fallen world the naked body has become a symbol of licentiousness and indignity. However, guided by Christ's words, John Paul challenges us in his theology of the body to realize that "from the beginning it was not so" (Mt 19:8).

**2a.** "In the first biblical draft of anthropology, [original nakedness] is not something accidental. On the contrary, it is precisely the key for its full and complete understanding" (52)

One of John Paul's main goals is to sketch a biblical anthropology — a vision of who we are as male and female. Original "nakedness without shame" is the key. Hence, the subtitle of these lectures.

- In the beginning, the naked body witnessed to Love, to purity, and to the sheer goodness of creation. It witnessed to "the glory of God" which "is man fully alive" (St. Irenaeus).
- In the rich symbolism of biblical language, the entrance of the fig leaves, then, marks an utter tragedy — the loss of purity, the loss of God's "full life" in man.

Yet the good news of the Gospel is that "Jesus came to restore creation to the purity of its origins" (CCC, n. 2336). He came so that we might once again have life, and have it to the full (see Jn 10:10).

- This *does not* mean that we are suddenly empowered to be "naked without shame."
- Even after baptism the effects of sin remain, as the ongoing battle for purity attests (see CCC, nn. 978, 1226, 1264, 1426).
- This inner struggle will not cease until the resurrection. Yet . . .

**2b.** "Even now [purity of heart] enables us to see *according to* God . . . ; it lets us perceive the human body — ours and our neighbor's — as a temple of the Holy Spirit, a manifestation of divine beauty" (CCC, n. 2519).

It is with this purity — with God's vision — that we seek to ponder the "great mystery" of the body.

## 3. Defining "Theology of the Body"

"Theology of the body" is the working title which John Paul gave to the 129 general audience addresses which make up the first major catechetical project of his pontificate. It is a biblical reflection on the meaning and experience of human embodiment and erotic desire.

**3a.** The theology of the body is "one of the boldest reconfigurations of Catholic theology in centuries" (WH, p. 336). It "has barely begun to shape the Church's theology, preaching, and religious education. When it does, it will compel a dramatic development of thinking about virtually every major theme in the Creed" (WH, p. 853)

**3b.** "These [129] catechetical addresses, taken together, constitute a kind of *theological time bomb* set to go off with dramatic consequences, sometime in the third millennium of the Church. When that happens, perhaps in the twenty-first century, the theology of the body may well be seen as a critical moment not only in Catholic theology, but in the history of modern thought" (WH, p. 343).

In Christian catechesis, people are used to an emphasis on the spiritual realm. However, many people are unfamiliar, and sometimes even uncomfortable, with a marked emphasis on the body. For John Paul, this is a false dichotomy. There is, without question, an ontological priority to the spirit. Yet,

**3c.** "As a being at once body and spirit, man expresses and perceives spiritual realities through physical signs and symbols." Man "needs signs and symbols to communicate with others. . . . The same holds true for his relationship with God" (CCC, n. 1146)

*Christianity does not reject the body!* In a virtual "ode to the flesh" the *Catechism* proclaims:

**3d.** "'The flesh is the hinge of salvation.' We believe in God who is creator of the flesh; we believe in the Word made flesh in order to redeem the flesh; we believe in the resurrection of the flesh, the fulfillment of both the creation and the redemption of the flesh" (CCC, n. 1015).

Far from devaluing the body, Catholicism is a very physical, sensual religion.

- It's through our bodily senses and the "stuff" of the material world that we most intimately encounter God.

- Through bathing the body with water, anointing the body with oil, eating and drinking the body and blood of Christ, the laying on of hands, confessing with our lips, and the "one flesh" reality of marriage, Christians encounter the divine mystery.

The human body itself is in some sense sacramental.

- This is a broader, more ancient understanding of the word "sacrament," meaning a sign which makes visible the invisible mystery of God.
- The body is the pre-eminent and primordial "sign" of the ultimate spiritual reality.
- It's from this perspective that John Paul wants to study the human body — not as biological organism, but as a *theology*, as a sign of the spiritual and divine mystery.

**3e.** "The body, in fact, and it alone, is capable of making visible what is invisible: the spiritual and divine. It was created to transfer into the visible reality of the world, the mystery hidden since time immemorial in God, and thus to be a sign of it" (76).

Since the entire catechesis hinges on this point, it's important to clarify what we mean (and don't mean) by speaking of the body as a "sign" of the divine mystery.

- A sign is something that points us to a reality beyond itself and, in some way, makes that transcendent reality present to us.
- The divine mystery always remains infinitely transcendent; it cannot be reduced to its sign. Yet the sign is indispensable in "making visible" the invisible mystery.

We must be careful not to blur the essential distinction between matter and spirit and (even more) creature and Creator. Yet, at the same time, we must affirm the profound unity between these.

- Christianity is the religion of the "great mystery" of God's union with humanity.
- It is the religion of the Word (pure Spirit) made flesh!
- God's mystery revealed in human flesh (theology *of the body*) — this is the very "logic" of Christianity.

**3f.** "Through the fact that the Word of God became flesh the body entered theology...through the main door" (89).

## 4. The "Nuptial Mystery" and the Spousal Analogy

What, then, is the divine mystery which the body signifies? It is the mystery of Trinitarian Life and Love — of Trinitarian *Communion* — and the plan "hidden for ages in God" (Eph 3:9) that man is destined in Christ to share in this eternal Communion.

**4a.** "God has revealed his innermost secret: God himself is an eternal exchange of love, Father, Son, and Holy Spirit, and he has destined us to share in that exchange" (CCC, n. 221).

What enables us to understand the body as a sign of this mystery?

- The beauty and mystery of sexual difference and the call to fruitful communion.
- Right from the beginning, this "great mystery" foreshadows the infinitely greater mystery of Christ's communion with the Church (see Eph 5:31-32).

**4b.** "The sacrament, as a visible sign, is constituted with man . . . by means of his 'visible' masculinity and femininity" (76).

Scripture employs many images to describe God's relationship with humanity. Each has its own valuable place. But the nuptial image is used most often and is favored by the greatest mystics.

- The Bible begins and ends with marriages — Adam-Eve and Christ-Church.
- Spousal theology looks to the nuptial "book ends" of Genesis and Revelation as a key for interpreting what lies between.
- Through the lens of the spousal analogy we learn that God's eternal plan is to espouse us to Himself forever (see Hos 2:19) — to "marry" us.
- God wanted this eternal plan of love and communion to be so obvious to us that he stamped an image of it in our very being by creating us as male and female.
- Whenever God establishes a covenant with man, we see the call to fruitful union — whether it is with Adam (Gn 1:28), Noah (Gn 9:1), Abraham (Gn 17:5-6), Jacob (Gn 35:10-12), or Moses (Lv 26:9).
- The signs of the Covenants also bear this nuptial mark.

**4c.** "*The Eucharist is the . . . sacrament of the Bridegroom and the Bride.*" It serves in some way "to express the relationship between man and woman, between what is 'feminine' and what is 'masculine.' It is a relationship willed by God in both the mystery of creation and in the mystery of Redemption" (MD, n. 26).

**4d.** "The Church cannot therefore be understood as the mystical body of Christ, as the sign of man's covenant with God in Christ, or as the universal sacrament of salvation, unless we keep in mind the 'great mystery' involved in the creation of man as male and female and the vocation of both to conjugal love, to fatherhood and to motherhood. The 'great mystery,' which is the Church and humanity in Christ, does not exist apart from the 'great mystery' expressed in the 'one flesh' ...reality of marriage and the family" (LF, n. 19).

While indicating a similarity, an analogy also indicates an *ever-greater dissimilarity*.

- We must be careful to maintain this substantial dissimilarity lest we move too continuously from creaturely life and communion to divine life and communion.
- This does not mean the analogy is extrinsic. It only means that we must always respect the mysterious and infinite difference between God and His creatures.

**4e.** "In no way is God in man's image. He is neither man nor woman. God is pure spirit in which there is no place for the difference between the sexes. But the respective 'perfections' of man and woman reflect something of the infinite perfection of God" (CCC, n. 370; see also nn. 42, 239).

NOTES

**4f.** "It is obvious that the analogy of earthly . . . spousal love cannot provide an adequate and complete understanding of . . . the divine mystery." It helps us "to understand it up to a certain point — naturally in an analogical way. . . . The mystery remains transcendent in regard to this analogy as in regard to any other analogy, whereby we seek to express it in human language. At the same time, however, this analogy offers the possibility of a certain . . . 'penetration' into the very essence of the mystery" (330).

## 5. The Great Divorce

If the body "and it alone" is capable of making the divine mystery visible to us, and if there is an enemy of God who wants to keep us from God's mystery, where might he go to counter God's plan?

- Satan seeks to counter God's plan by plagiarizing the sacraments (Tertullian). Where better to begin than with the "primordial sacrament"?
- It is no coincidence that St. Paul follows his presentation of the "great mystery" of nuptial union (Eph 5) with the call to take up arms in the cosmic struggle between good and evil (Eph 6).
- The battle for man's soul is always fought over the primordial truth of his body. St. Paul's first words of advice: "gird your loins with the truth" (Eph 6:14).
- How do we recognize the anti-Christ? It is the one who denies Christ come in the flesh (see 1 Jn 4:2-3).

If we're looking for that which is most sacred, all we need do is look for that which is most often and most violently profaned. We see here a great clash between the "symbolic" and the "diabolic."

- In the Greek, *symbalein* means to bring together, gather up, unite.
- *Diabolein* means to scatter, break apart, rupture.
- God's eternal plan for the body is union, communion, marriage; this brings life.
- Satan's counter-plan for the body is separation, fracture, divorce; this brings death.

A fallen world, then, is a world of estranged spouses: estrangement between divinity and humanity; heaven and earth; soul and body; spirituality and sexuality; sacredness and sensuality; masculinity and femininity.

← DUALISM →

angelism
prudery rigorism
repression

animalism
indecency permissivism
indulgence

History has oscillated between these two polarities. The solution is not to swing the pendulum to the other extreme, but to find integration, unity of body and soul, sexuality and spirituality. Christ — through the very dynamism of the Incarnation and paschal mystery — heals the rift.

**5a.** "The truth is that only in the mystery of incarnate Word does the mystery of man take on light. . . . Christ, the final Adam, by the revelation of the mystery of the Father and his love, fully reveals man to himself and makes his supreme calling clear" (GS, n. 22).

**5b.** "The Redeemer of man, Jesus Christ, is the center of the universe and of history" (RH, n. 1).

The need for man to "discover his true (integrated) self" could not be any more pressing. The stakes are incredibly high. Indeed Karol Wojtyla knows well that a dualistic anthropology leads man to the gas chamber, to the abortion mill, to the culture of death.

## 6. The Root of Ethics and Culture

John Paul II has become such a champion of human life, dignity, and freedom precisely because of the crucible of death, degradation, and tyranny in which he was formed. Through the horrors of Nazi occupation and Communist Poland, Wojtyla wrestled with God in search of answers to the hardest of life's questions. What could lead man who is bestowed with God-like dignity to drink from the dregs of raw evil? He was not interested in surface solutions. He wanted to go to the root of it all.

What is that root? Summarizing the thought of the Holy Father, it is our rejection of God's revelation of love that He *inscribed in our bodies*.

**6a.** The call to nuptial love and communion inscribed in our masculine and feminine bodies is "the fundamental element of human existence in the world" (16), "the foundation of human life" (EM, 46), and, hence, "the deepest substratum of human ethics and culture"(163).

**6b.** The common life of men and women "constitutes the pure and simple fabric of existence." Thus, "human life, . . . its dignity, its balance, depend, at every moment of history and at every point of geographical longitude and latitude, on 'who' she will be for him and he for her" (159).

**6c.** Confusion about sexual morality "involves a danger perhaps greater than is generally realized: the danger of confusing the basic and fundamental human tendencies, the main paths of human existence. Such confusion must clearly affect the whole spiritual position of man" (LR, p. 66).

**6d.** "'God gave them up in the lusts of their hearts to impurity' (Ro 1:24), from which there also comes all moral disorder." The impurity of lust "distorts both sexual life (see Ro 1:24-27) and the operation of social and economic life (see Ro 1:29-32)" (230-231).

**6e.** The "conjugal union . . . is the *natural* foundation, as well as the ontological core, of the family" (PC, p. 339).

**6f.** "It is an illusion to think we can build a true culture of human life if we do not . . . accept and experience sexuality and love and the whole of life according to their true meaning and their close inter-connection" (EV, n. 97).

**6g.** The "choices and the actions [of men and women] take on all the weight of human existence in the union of the two" (376).

## 7. Structure of the Catechesis

This is why John Paul's first major catechetical project (even before his extended catechesis on the Creed) was devoted to developing a biblical vision of sexual love.

The theology of the body was inspired by Paul VI's call for a "total vision of man" in his controversial encyclical *Humana Vitae*. By sketching this "total vision" (what John Paul calls an "adequate anthropology"), John Paul shifts the discussion from "How far can I go?" to "What does it mean to be human?" "Why did God create us male and female in the first place?"

PART I: Establishing an "Adequate Anthropology"
(Who are we as male and female?)

- Original Man
- Historical Man
- Eschatological Man

PART II: Applying an "Adequate Anthropology"
(How are we supposed to live?)

- Celibacy for the Kingdom
- The Sacramentality of Marriage
- Love and Fruitfulness (a reflection on *Humanae Vitae*)

It's very important to realize that this is not merely a catechesis on sex and marriage.

- If we stay the course, curiosity about the meaning of the body and of sexuality — so often considered innately prurient — actually leads us into the heart of the Christian mystery and the meaning of our humanity.
- We mustn't be misled by the term "theology of the body" as if it were only "part" of an adequate anthropology (as if we needed to add to this a "theology of the soul").
- The uniqueness of the Pope's project is the assertion that a "total vision of man" must be a theology of the body.

**7a.** What we learn is obviously "important in regard to marriage and the Christian vocation of husbands and wives." However it "is equally essential and valid for the understanding of man in general: for the fundamental problem of understanding him and for the self-comprehension of his being in the world" (352-353).

**7b.** Even in its limited scope, the Pope's catechesis on the body affords "the rediscovery of the meaning of the whole of existence, the meaning of life" (168). Therefore, "it is this theology of the body which is the basis of the most suitable method of the . . . education (in fact the self-education) of man" (215).

**7c.** "The theology of the body is not merely a theory, but rather a specific, evangelical, Christian pedagogy of the body" (396). "When we speak of the meaning of the body, we refer in the first place to the full awareness of the human being" (124).

**7d.** Understanding Christ's revelation regarding the human body and its redemption "concerns the entire Bible" (249). It plunges us into "the perspective of the whole Gospel, of the whole teaching, in fact, of the whole mission of Christ" (175).

## 8. A Word on the Pope's Philosophical Project

Modern philosophy has focused on *subjectivity* to the neglect of *objectivity* and, thus, has erred by divorcing freedom from truth. At the same time modern philosophy has challenged men like Wojtyla to recognize that traditional formulations of the faith may well have focused on objectivity to the neglect of subjectivity. To the modern mind, traditional formulations of the faith can seem abstract.

Wojtyla's philosophical project has been to forge a link between objective reality and subjective human experience. Just as Augustine integrated his synthesis of the faith with the philosophy of Plato, and Aquinas with Aristotle, Karol Wojtyla/John Paul II inaugurates a new era for the Church by integrating his synthesis of the faith with phenomenology.

*Phenomenology* seeks to retrieve the ordinary experiences of everyday life and study these phenomena *as we experience them* and, in this way, approach the reality of things-as-they-are.

- With human experience as a point of departure, Wojtyla discovers in the subjectivity of man's inner-world a unity with the objectivity of man's outer-world.
- By pressing into this unity he is able to confirm objective truths while avoiding "objectivizing" abstractions.
- He is able to demonstrate that the Church's vision of man is not foisted upon him from "the outside," but corresponds to his self-experience as a person on "the inside."
- Thus, Wojtyla does not need to force assent to his proposals through rigorous, logical argumentation. Rather, he solicits men and women to reflect honestly on their own self-experience to see if his proposals are confirmed there.

In short, if the traditional philosophy of being tends to address the "God question" by providing rational proofs for His existence, Wojtyla's philosophical project tends to address the same question by inviting each person to "taste and see."

- In this way "proof" of God's existence is verified not only in the mind but even more so in the heart.
- People understand a concept with the mind, but people love persons with the heart.

**8a.** "And we find ourselves by now very close to Saint Thomas, but the path passes not so much through being and existence as through people and their meeting each other, through the 'I" and the 'Thou.'. . . In the *sphere of the everyday* man's entire life is one of 'coexistence' — 'thou' and 'I' — and also in the *sphere of the absolute and definitive*: 'I' and 'THOU'" (CTH, p. 36).

The cry that the Church "just isn't 'in touch' with real life experience" is heard especially in regard to sexual ethics.

- Church pronouncements on sexual matters have traditionally focused mainly on the exterior "duties" of spouses, and the objective "ends" of the sexual act.
- Attention seemed almost fixated on the "primary end" of procreation with little to no attention given to the meaning and inner experience of conjugal love.
- Objectively speaking, the traditional formulation on the ends of marriage is true. But for most people today, focusing merely on the objective reality tends to create a "disconnect" with the interior experience of the persons involved.

John Paul's "*personalism*" treats ethical questions from this "insider's" perspective. This approach does not separate us from objective truth as some imagine. Rather, through his explicit appeal to personal experience, the Holy Father provides "subjective resonance" for objective norms.

**8b.** "In this renewed formulation, the traditional teaching on the purposes of marriage (and their hierarchy) is reaffirmed and at the same time deepened from the viewpoint of the interior life of the spouses" (407).

**8c.** "Sexual morality is within the domain of the person. It is impossible to understand anything about it without understanding what a person is. The personal order is the only proper plane for all debate on matters of sexual morality" (LR, p. 18).

**8d.** *The Personalistic Norm* states, in its negative form, that persons are the kind of beings that do not admit of being used. In its positive form it states that the only proper response to a person is love (see LR, p. 41).

NOTES

# PART I

## Who Are We?

## *Establishing an Adequate Anthropology*

NOTES

# Cycle 1: Original Man

(TB, pp. 25-102)

This cycle consists of 23 general audience addresses delivered between September 5, 1979 and April 2, 1980. Here John Paul reflects upon the body, sexuality, and marriage as man and woman experienced them "in the beginning" before sin. We must return to our "beginnings" (our theological "prehistory") if we are to understand who we are as God intended us to be. This is the first element in the "triptych" that makes up John Paul's "adequate anthropology" — his "total vision of man."

## 1. Christ Points Us Back to "the Beginning"

"For your hardness of heart Moses allowed you to divorce your wives, but from the beginning it was not so" (Mt 19:8).

- By beginning with the words of Christ, John Paul is making a specific anthropological statement: "Christ fully reveals man to himself."
- The "boundary" between original man and historical man cannot, in all actuality, be crossed. Yet Christ orders us in some sense to go "beyond" the boundary (see 31).
- Christ, through the "redemption of the body" reestablishes the beginning as the norm.
- Christ helps historical man to view the "beginning" (original man) as his true fullness and the gift of salvation gives birth to the hope of returning to the beginning at the end (eschatological man) as a sort of homecoming.

**1a.** The "first man and the first woman must constitute the beginning and the model of that communion for all men and women who, in any period, are united so intimately as to be 'one flesh'" (50).

**1b.** There is "*an essential continuity and a link* between these two different states or dimensions of the human being." The historical state "plunges its roots, in every man without any exception, in his own theological 'prehistory,' which is the state of original innocence" (32).

**1c.** "Historical man tries to understand the mystery of original innocence almost by means of a contrast" (68).

In the full context of Christ's words, he refers to both creation accounts: the Elohist account of Genesis 1 (objective) and the Yahwist account of Genesis 2 and 3 (subjective).

## 2. Original Human Experiences

Examining human experience is indispensable in constructing the theology of the body.

- John Paul seeks to "reconstruct" man's original experiences not so much to determine who man and woman were "then," as to help us understand *who we are now*.
- In the final analysis, we can't determine the "prehistorical" events and experiences with "historical" certainty. We approach them only through "the symbolism of biblical language" (CCC, n. 375).

**2a.** The biblical "language in question is a mythical one." However, "the term 'myth' does not designate a fabulous content, but merely an archaic way of expressing a deeper content" (43).

**2b.** "In the interpretation of the revelation about man, and especially about the body, we must, for understandable reasons, refer to experience, since corporeal man is perceived by us mainly by experience" (34). "We have the right, therefore, to speak of the relationship between experience and revelation." Without this we ponder only "abstract considerations rather than man as a living subject" (94).

**2c.** "Speaking of original human experiences, we have in mind not so much their distance in time, as rather their basic significance." These experiences "are always at the root of every human experience. . . . They are, in fact, so intermingled with the ordinary things of life that we do not generally notice their extraordinary character" (51).

John Paul focuses on three "original human experiences" in the state of man's original innocence: *original solitude*, *original unity*, and *original nakedness*.

## 3. Original Solitude: The First Discovery of Personhood

"Then the Lord God said, 'It is not good that the man should be alone; I will make him a helper fit for him'" (Gn 2:18).

- Means not only that man is "alone" without woman (and woman without man), but that man (the human being) is "alone" in the visible world as a *person*.
- He discovers in naming the animals that he alone is aware of himself and is able to determine his own actions. He alone can "name" and "till."
- Man's freedom is fully revealed in the alternative between death and immortality.
- Man discovers that he is a "partner of the Absolute" and a "subject of the covenant."
- In short, solitude determines that man stands alone in the visible world as a creature made in God's image. He is a "body," but he cannot be reduced to the visible world.
- Solitude points to the spiritual aspects of man's nature, but is discovered through the experience of his body. The body expresses man's difference from the animals, his subjectivity, and his call to communion with God and with an "other" like himself.

**3a.** The man "might have reached the conclusion, on the basis of the experience of his own body, that he was substantially similar to the other living beings (*animalia*). But, on the contrary, . . . he reached the conviction that he was 'alone'" (39).

**3b.** The "body expresses the person. It is, therefore, in all its materiality, almost penetrable and transparent, in such a way as to make it clear who man is (and who he should be)" (41).

**3c.** Solitude "signifies man's subjectivity, which is constituted through self-knowledge." Man's self-knowledge "develops at the same rate as knowledge of the visible world, . . . of all the living beings to which man has given a name to affirm his own dissimilarity with regard to them." This is man's "first act of self-consciousness" through which he "asserts himself as a 'person' in the visible world" (37).

**3d.** The experience of original solitude helps us understand that "corporality and sexuality are not completely identified" (43). Solitude is "a fundamental anthropological problem, prior, in a certain sense, to the one raised by the fact that this man is male and female. This problem is prior not so much in the chronological sense . . . : it is prior 'by its very nature'" (36). Therefore, the fact that "man is a 'body' belongs to the structure of the personal subject more deeply than the fact that he is in his somatic constitution also male or female" (43).

## 4. The Creation of Woman

"So the Lord God caused a deep sleep to fall upon the man, and while he slept took one of his ribs and . . . made [it] into a woman. . . . . Then the man said, 'This at last is bone of my bones and flesh of my flesh" (Gn 2:21-23).

- In order for two creatures to enter communion (original unity), they must first be the kind of beings capable of communion (original solitude).
- "Double solitude" (two persons who share the same solitude), then, is the indispensable foundation of original unity.
- Double solitude is also the sure foundation of the true equality of man and woman.
- Adam's "deep sleep" indicates his return to non-being and God's "recreation" of man as male and female.
- The woman's creation from the rib is an "archaic, metaphorical, and figurative way" of expressing the fact that they share the same humanity (see 44).
- Bones for the Jews signified the whole human being (see 96).

**4a.** There "is no doubt that man falls into that 'sleep' with the desire of finding a being like himself. . . . In this way the solitude of the man-person is broken, because the first 'man' awakens from his sleep as 'male and female'" (44).

**4b.** Adam's words "express wonder and admiration, even more, the sense of fascination"(369). "Exclaiming in this way, he seems to say: here is *a body that expresses the 'person'*" (61).

**4c.** Masculinity and femininity are "two 'incarnations' of the same . . . solitude, before God and the world — two ways . . . of 'being a body' and at the same time a man." Masculinity and femininity "complete each other." They are "two complementary ways of being conscious of the meaning of the body" (48).

**4d.** Sex "is, in a sense, 'a constituent part of the person' (not just 'an attribute of the person'). . . . The presence of the feminine element, along side the male element and together with it, signifies an enrichment for man in the whole perspective of his history, including the history of salvation" (49).

If men and women are to "find themselves," the solitude of every "he" or "she" must lead to the communion of a human "we." If every*body* is "alone" as a person, every*body* also needs a "helper."

**4e.** The "norm of existence as a person is shown . . . precisely by means of the meaning of these two words: 'alone' and 'helper'" (60-61). Therefore, to be a person "means both 'being subject' and 'being in relationship'" (371).

## 5. Original Unity: The Communion of Persons

"Therefore a man leaves his father and his mother and cleaves to his wife, and they become one flesh" (Gn 2:24).

- Original unity overcomes solitude (in the sense of being alone without the "other") and affirms everything about man's solitude (in the sense that he is a person).
- Thus, original unity also reveals that man is different from the animals, that male and female are created in the image and likeness of God.
- John Paul defines the original unity as a "communion of persons."

**5a.** Communion "is *a mode of being and acting in mutual relation to one another* (not just 'in common' with another) *such that through this . . . they mutually confirm and affirm one another as persons*" (PC, p. 321).

**5b.** Becoming "one flesh" refers not only to the joining of two bodies but is "a 'sacramental' expression which corresponds to the communion of persons" (123).

**5c.** "Man becomes the image of God not so much in the moment of solitude as in the moment of communion." In other words, man images God "not only through his own humanity, but also through the communion of persons which man and woman form right from the beginning." This "constitutes, perhaps, the deepest theological aspect of all that can be said about man. . . . On all this, right from the beginning, there descended the blessing of fertility linked with human procreation" (46).

**5d.** The "one flesh" unity of which Genesis 2:24 speaks "is undoubtedly what is expressed and realized in the conjugal act. The biblical formulation . . . does not permit us to stop at the surface of human sexuality . . . but obliges us right from the beginning to see the fullness and depth characteristic of this unity" (49). This fullness and depth "is the pure and simple truth of communion between persons" (61).

**5e.** "In marriage, the physical intimacy of the spouses becomes a sign and pledge of spiritual communion" (CCC, n. 2360).

**5f.** "It is not sexuality which creates in a man and a woman the need to give themselves to each other, but, on the contrary, it is the need to give oneself, latent in every human person, which finds its outlet . . . in physical and sexual union, in matrimony. But the need . . . to give oneself to and unite with another person is deeper and connected with the spiritual existence of the person. It is not finally and completely satisfied simply by union with another human being. Considered in the perspective of the person's eternal existence, marriage is only a tentative solution of the problem of a union of persons through love" (LR, pp. 253-254).

**5g.** In "every conjugal union of man and woman . . . there is renewed, in a way, the mystery of creation in all its original depth and vital power." "Man and woman uniting with each other (in the conjugal act) . . . return in that way to that union in humanity ('flesh of my flesh and bone of my bones') which allows them to recognize each other and, like the first time, to call each other by name. This means reliving, in a sense, the original virginal value of man which emerges from the mystery of his solitude before God" (49, 50).

**5h.** In "the entire Bible," Genesis 2:24 (the two become one flesh) "can be considered the fundamental text on marriage" (321). These are "the words that constitute the sacrament of marriage" (76) and they "will have in the revelation of God an ample and distant perspective. This unity through the body ('and the two will be one flesh') possesses . . . an ethical dimension . . . and also a sacramental dimension" (47).

## 6. Original Nakedness: Key to Biblical Anthropology

"And the man and his wife were both naked, and were not ashamed" (Gn 2:25).

- Genesis 2:25 penetrates the subjective experience of man and woman with precision.
- Original nakedness shows full awareness of the original meaning of the body as the revelation of the person.
- Original nakedness indicates a total defenselessness before the other, an absence of barriers, because of a total trust in the sincerity of their mutual exchange.
- This "original innocence of knowledge" (see 56) demonstrates a total unity between the spiritual and the physical.
- "The deepest desire of the human heart is to see another and be seen by that other" (St. Augustine).

**6a.** "In the first biblical draft of anthropology, [original nakedness] is not something accidental. On the contrary, it is precisely the key for its full and complete understanding" (52).

**6b.** "This seeing each other is not just a participation in [an] 'exterior' perception of the world, but has also an interior dimension of participation in the vision of the Creator Himself. . . . 'Nakedness signifies the original good of God's vision. It signifies all the simplicity and fullness of the vision through which the 'pure' value of humanity as male and female, the 'pure' value of the body and of sex, is manifested (57).

**6c.** They "see and know each other, in fact, with all the peace of the interior gaze, which creates precisely the fullness of the intimacy of persons" (57).

**6d.** The "words of Genesis 2:25 . . . express the fact that, together with man, holiness entered the visible world." It is "in his body as male or female [that] man feels he is a subject of holiness." Holiness is what "enables man to express himself deeply with his own body . . . precisely by means of the 'sincere gift' of himself" (76-77).

**6e.** "Only the nakedness that makes woman an 'object' for the man, or vice versa, is a source of shame. The fact that 'they were not ashamed' means that the woman was not an 'object' for the man nor he for her" (75).

## 7. The Reality of the Gift

In God's declaration of the goodness of creation, we recognize that His motive for creating is love. God desires for man to share in His own life. This is the utterly gratuitous "gift" of creation.

- God initiates His own self-gift by creating us in His image and for "our own sakes."
- In the original covenant, man receives this gift and gives himself back to God.

- Man and woman image and recapitulate the gift of God in creation by becoming a gift to each other.
- Living the gift is a participation in "grace."

**7a.** "God has no other reason for creating than his love and goodness" (CCC, n. 293).

**7b.** "The dimension of the gift decides the essential truth and depth of meaning of the original solitude-unity-nakedness" (58).

**7c.** "This is the body: a witness to creation as a fundamental gift, and so a witness to Love as the source from which this same giving springs. . . . Such is the meaning with which sex enters the theology of the body" (62).

**7d.** "Man appears in the visible world as the highest expression of the divine gift, because he bears within himself the interior dimension of the gift" (76).

**7e.** The "concept of 'giving' cannot refer to a nothingness. It indicates the one who gives, and the one who receives the gift, and also the relationship that is established between them" (59).

**7f.** The term "'nuptial' . . . manifests in a word the whole reality of that donation of which the first pages of the Book of Genesis speak to us" (66).

**7g.** If "creation is a gift to man, then his fullness and deepest dimension is determined by grace, that is, by participation in the interior life of God Himself, in His holiness" (67).

**7h.** Holiness "is measured according to the 'great mystery' in which the Bride responds with the gift of love to the gift of the Bridegroom" (MD, n. 27; CCC, n. 773).

## 8. The Nuptial Meaning of the Body

The body's "nuptial meaning" is revealed by God and at the same time "discovered" by man in Genesis 2:23-25.

- The "interior" dimension of the gift also has an "exterior" reality.
- The spiritual call to be a gift — to love as God loves — is stamped in the beauty and mystery of the body in its sexual complementarity.

**8a.** "It follows then, that if man is the only creature on earth that God willed for its own sake, man can fully discover his true self only in a sincere giving of himself" (GS, n. 24).

**8b.** "Every man and every woman fully realizes himself or herself through the sincere gift of self. For spouses, the moment of conjugal union constitutes a very particular expression of this. It is then that a man and a woman . . . become a mutual gift to each other" (LF, n. 12).

**8c.** The nuptial meaning of the body is the body's "capacity of expressing love: that love precisely in which the man-person becomes a gift and — by means of this gift — fulfills the very meaning of his being and existence" (63).

**8d.** The nuptial meaning of the body also indicates "the capacity and deep availability for the 'affirmation of the person.'" This "is nothing but acceptance of the gift, which, by means of reciprocity, creates the communion of persons" (65).

**8e.** The nuptial meaning of the body "is the fundamental element of human existence in the world" (66).

**8f.** Man "will never avoid this indispensable 'theme' of his own existence. . . . In fact, in the whole perspective of his own 'history,' man will not fail to confer a nuptial meaning on his own body. Even if this meaning undergoes and will undergo many distortions, it will always remain [at] the deepest level . . . as a sign of the 'image of God.' The way that goes from the mystery of creation to the 'redemption of the body' (see Ro 8) also passes here" (65-66).

NOTES

## 9. The Freedom of the Gift

Sexual desire was not experienced as a compulsive urge, but as the desire to make a sincere gift of self — to love as God loves. It was an experience permeated by grace.

- The freedom of the gift indicates that man and woman respected one another as persons who were created for their "own sakes."
- If they were to live in communion, they had to bestow the gift of self freely. They could not grasp or possess one another. They could not "extort the gift."
- Freedom, as we shall learn, is our capacity for heaven.

**9a.** Man and woman are both naked without shame "because they are free with the very freedom of the gift. This freedom lies precisely at the basis of the nuptial meaning of the body" (63).

**9b.** "We mean here freedom particularly as mastery of oneself (self control)." Such freedom "is indispensable in order that man . . . may become a gift, in order that . . . he will be able to 'fully discover his true self' in 'a sincere giving of himself'" (64).

**9c.** Grace is "that mysterious gift made to the inner man — to the human 'heart' — which enables . . . man and woman to exist from the 'beginning' in the mutual relationship of the disinterested gift of oneself"(68).

## 10. Original Happiness

Refers to the original beatifying (supremely happy, blissful) experience of man and woman's communion with God and with each other. This foreshadows (even if only dimly) the beatifying communion of heaven.

**10a.** "The revelation and discovery of the nuptial meaning of the body explain man's original happiness" (65).

**10b.** "Happiness is being rooted in love. Original happiness speaks to us of the 'beginning' of man who emerged from Love and initiated love. . . . This 'beginning' can also be defined as the beatifying immunity from shame as the result of love" (67).

## 11. The Primordial Sacrament

Since the "one flesh" reality of marriage refers right from the beginning to the "great mystery" of Christ's union with the Church, John Paul describes marriage as the *primordial sacrament*.

- All of creation is sacramental in that it reveals something of the mystery of its Creator.
- But this "sacramentality of the world" reaches its fulfillment (or crown) in man created in the image of God as male and female.
- Man, in turn, reaches his fulfillment through the sincere gift of self which was realized in an original way through the incarnate union of Genesis 2:24.

**11a.** "In the primordial awareness of the nuptial meaning of the body, pervaded by the mystery of original innocence . . . there is constituted a primordial sacrament understood as a sign that transmits effectively in the visible world the invisible mystery hidden in God from time immemorial. And this is the mystery of truth and love, the mystery of divine life, in which man really participates" (76).

**11b.** "The sacrament, as a visible sign, is constituted with man as a 'body' by means of his 'visible' masculinity and femininity. The body, in fact, and it alone is capable of making visible what is invisible: the spiritual and divine. It was created to transfer into the visible reality of the world the mystery hidden since time immemorial in God, and thus to be a sign of it" (76).

**11c.** God "impressed his own form on the flesh . . . in such a way that even what was visible might bear the divine form" (CCC, n. 704).

**11d.** "Against this vast background we understand fully those words that constitute the sacrament of marriage, present in Genesis 2:24 ('A man leaves his father and his mother and cleaves to his wife, and they become one flesh')" (76).

## 12. The Knowledge-Generation Cycle

"Adam knew his wife Eve, and she conceived . . ." (Gn 4:1).

- "Knowledge" refers to the profound discovery of life's meaning in the gift of self.
- In the "knowledge-generation cycle," the goodness of human life and of the sexual relationship continues to assert itself despite the tragedy of sin and death.
- Knowledge leads to a "third" who shares the same divine image as his parents.
- It is the woman, in her exaltation "I have gotten a man with the help of the Lord" (Gn 4:1) who expresses the whole theological depth of procreation.

**12a.** "The Bible (and subsequently the liturgy) . . . honors and praises throughout the centuries 'the womb that bore you and the breasts that you sucked' (Lk 11:27). These words constitute a eulogy of motherhood, of femininity, of the female body in its typical expression of creative love" (82).

**12b.** "Speaking here of 'knowledge,' . . . the Bible indicates the deepest essence of married life" (79).

**12c.** "The term 'knew' synthesizes the whole density of the biblical text analyzed so far. . . . Everyone finds himself again in his own way, in that biblical 'knowledge'" (80, 81).

**12d.** "Sin and death entered Man's history, in a way, through the very heart of that unity which, from 'the beginning,' was formed by man and woman, created and called to become 'one flesh'" (77).

**12e.** "Awareness of the [nuptial] meaning of the body and . . . of its generative meaning come into contact, in man, with awareness of death. . . . Yet there always returns in the history of man the 'knowledge-generation' cycle, in which life struggles, ever anew, with the inexorable perspective of death, and always overcomes it" (85-86).

**12f.** "Man, in spite of all the experiences of his life, in spite of sufferings, disappointment with himself, his sinfulness, and, finally, in spite of the inevitable prospect of death, always continues, however, to put 'knowledge' at the 'beginning' of 'generation.' In this way he seems to participate in that first vision of God himself: behold, it is very good" (86).

 NOTES

# Cycle 2: Historical Man

(TB, pp. 103-232)

This cycle consists of 40 general audience addresses delivered between April 16, 1980 and May 6, 1981. Here John Paul reflects upon the body, sexuality, and marriage as man (male and female) experiences them in history influenced by sin. Historical man, however, is not merely the man influenced by sin. He is also the man redeemed in Christ Jesus. This is the second element in the "triptych" that makes up John Paul's "adequate anthropology."

## 1. Adultery in the Heart

"You have heard that it was said, 'You shall not commit adultery.' But I say to you that everyone who looks at a woman lustfully has already committed adultery with her in his heart" (Mt 5:27-28).

- The heart is man's deep interior self where he experiences the forces of good and evil fighting and competing against each other.
- The heart is where we know and experience the true meaning of the body, or, because of the hardness of our hearts, fail to do so.
- Christ's words are not so much a condemnation of the human heart, but a calling. . . .
- They show "how deep down it is necessary to go" to fulfill the law of the Gospel (see 158).

**1a.** "Are we to fear the severity of [Christ's] words, or rather have confidence in their salvific content, in their power?" (159).

**1b.** The man who lets these words act in him "will be able to hear within him . . . almost the echo of that 'beginning,' that good 'beginning' to which Christ refers on another occasion" (167).

**1c.** The heritage of our hearts "is deeper than the sinfulness inherited, deeper than lust. . . . The words of Christ . . . reactivate that deeper heritage and give it real power in man's life" (168).

**1d.** "Christ in this case wants to bring out that the man 'looks' in conformity with what he is" (147). Lust changes "the intentionality of man's very existence" (150).

**1e.** Christ's words "demand, so to speak, that man enter his full image" (107). Man "must perceive anew the lost fullness of his humanity and want to regain it" (159).

**1f.** "Christ, in the Sermon on the Mount, . . . assigns as a duty to every man the dignity of every woman. And in an indirect way "He also assigns to every woman the dignity of every man. Finally, he assigns to everyone — both to man and woman — their own dignity . . . in consideration of their masculinity or femininity." Upholding this dignity "is assigned as an ethos to every man, male and female; it is assigned to his 'heart,' to his conscience, to his looks, and to his behavior" (346, 347).

## 2. Ethic and Ethos

"Unless your righteousness exceeds that of the scribes and the Pharisees, you will never enter the kingdom of heaven" (Mt 5:20). "You blind Pharisee! First cleanse the inside of the cup and of the plate, that the outside also may be clean" (Mt 23:26).

- We all know it is possible to follow rules without ever attaining holiness. It's called "legalism" or "moralism."
- "Ethos" refers to a person's inner world of values, what attracts and repulses him.
- In effect, Christ's teaching about lust expresses this: "You've heard the objective law and what it calls you to *externally*. Now I tell you what this means subjectively — what it calls you to *internally*."
- In other words, "You've heard the *ethic*. Now I tell you the *ethos*."
- In the new "ethos of redemption," through ongoing conversion of heart, the subjective desires of the heart gradually come in harmony with the objective norm.

**2a.** Ethos "can be defined as the interior form, almost the soul, of human morality. . . . To reach it, it is not enough to stop 'at the surface' of human actions, it is necessary to penetrate inside" (104, 105).

**2b.** "Christ not only confirms [the] essential ethical content of the commandment, but aims at strengthening it in the very depth of the human person. The new dimension of *ethos* is always connected with the revelation of that depth, which is called 'heart,' and with its liberation from 'lust'" (158).

**2c.** "Christian ethos is characterized by a transformation of the conscience and attitudes of the human person, both man and woman, such as to express and realize the value of the body and sex according to the Creator's original plan, placed as they are in the service of the 'communion of persons'" (163).

**2d.** The ethos of redemption is "a living morality . . . in which there is realized the very meaning of being a man" (105).

**2e.** "The perfection of the moral good consists in man's being moved to the good not only by his will but also by his 'heart'" and even "by his sensitive appetite" (CCC, n. 1770, 1775). "All Christ's faithful are to direct their affections rightly" (CCC, n. 2545).

**2f.** "It is impossible to keep the Lord's commandment by imitating the divine model from outside; there has to be a vital participation, coming from the depths of the heart" (CCC, n. 2842).

## 3. Fulfillment of the Law and Freedom from It

"Think not that I have come to abolish the law and the prophets. I have come not to abolish them, *but to fulfill them*" (Mt 5:17). If "you are led by the Spirit, you are not under the law" (Gal 5:18).

- We all know that laws, in and of themselves, do not change human hearts.
- Christ did not come to give us more "rules" to follow, but to change our hearts so that we could "fulfill the law."

- Fulfilling the law does not only mean meeting the laws demands externally.
- In effect Christ says, "You've heard the commandment not to commit adultery, but the problem is you *desire* to commit adultery."
- In as much as a person is "led by the Spirit" he no longer needs an objective norm constraining him from committing adultery. He *does not desire* to commit adultery.
- Such a person is free from the law. Lust — even if he is still capable of it — no longer holds sway in his heart.

**3a.** Christian ethos "is at the same time the fulfillment of the law by means of the 'superabounding' of justice" in man's heart. This forms a proper "interior perception of values" and "makes us enter the depth of the norm itself" (105).

**3b.** The Law "does not of itself give the strength, the grace of the spirit, to fulfill it. Because of sin, which it cannot remove, it remains a law of bondage" (CCC, n. 1963).
**3c.** "The Law of the Gospel . . . does not add new external precepts, but proceeds to reform the heart, the root of human acts, where man chooses between the pure and the impure" (CCC, n. 1968).

**3d.** In the Sermon on the Mount "the Spirit of the Lord gives new form to our desires, those inner movements that animate our lives" (CCC, n. 2764).

## 4. Questioning the Gift

"You will not die. For God knows that when you eat of it your eyes will be opened, and you will be like God, knowing good and evil" (Gn 3:4-5).

- When God is conceived as a jealous tyrant, man is goaded to do battle against Him so as not to be enslaved.
- Faith leads to "receptivity" before God. Lack of faith leads to "grasping."
- When we deny the gift in God, we lose our capacity to be a gift to one another.

**4a.** Woman "is the representative and the archetype of the whole human race: she *represents the humanity* which belongs to all human beings, both men and women" (MD, n. 4).

**4b.** The "paradigm of master-slave is foreign to the Gospel" (CTH, p. 226).

**4c.** "Questioning in his heart the deepest meaning of the donation, that is, love as the specific motive of the creation and of the original covenant, man turns his back on God-Love, on 'the Father.' In a way, he casts Him out of his heart" (111).

**4d.** "*This is truly the key for interpreting reality. . . . Original sin, then, attempts to abolish fatherhood*" (CTH, p. 228).

**4e.** "Christ, *through the revelation of the mystery of the Father and his love*, fully reveals man to himself and makes his supreme calling clear" (GS, n. 22; emphasis added).

**4f.** If original sin is the denial of the gift, "*faith*, in its deepest essence, is *the openness* of the human heart to the gift: *to God's self-communication in the Holy Spirit*" (DV, n. 51).

## 5. The Entrance of Shame

"Then the eyes of both were opened, and they knew that they were naked; and they sewed fig leaves together and made themselves aprons. . . . 'I was afraid, because I was naked; and I hid myself (Gn 3:7, 10).

- This shows "the frontier" between original man and historical man.
- Nakedness once revealed participation in holiness/grace, now it reveals their loss.
- Man loses the freedom of the gift and purity of heart.
- We no longer see the body as the revelation of the person and of the divine "gift."
- The body and gender difference are now "blamed" for the rupture caused by sin, but this is a "cover up" — almost an "excuse" not to face the disorder of the heart.

**5a.** Shame is so acute as to cause a "fundamental disquiet in the whole of human existence" (115).

**5b.** "Shame has a double meaning: it indicates the threat to the value [of the person] and at the same time preserves this value interiorly" (117). Thus, shame in this positive and protective sense "is a permanent element of culture and morals" (222).

**5c.** Shame "is a natural *form of self-defense for the person* against the danger of descending or being pushed into the position of an object for sexual use" (LR, p. 182).

**5d.** "There is imprinted on this shame . . . a certain 'echo' of man's original innocence itself: a 'negative' . . . of the image, whose 'positive' had been precisely original innocence" (204).

**5e.** With the entrance of shame, it is as if man "felt that he had just stopped . . . being above the world of living beings or 'animalia.' It is as if he felt a specific break of the personal integrity of his own body, particularly in what determines its sexuality" (116).

**5f.** Shame enters when man "realizes for the first time that his body has ceased drawing upon the power of the spirit, which raised him to the level of the image of God" (115).

**5g.** "Man is ashamed of his body because of lust. In fact, he is ashamed not so much of his body as precisely of lust" (116)

**5h.** Purity of heart affords "'the absorption of shame by love.' Shame is, as it were, swallowed up by love, dissolved in it, so that the man and the woman are no longer ashamed to be sharing their experience of sexual values. This process is enormously important to sexual morality." This "does not mean that [shame (in its positive sense)] is eliminated or destroyed. Quite the contrary, it is reinforced." Yet where there is genuine love, shame (in the negative sense) "as the natural way of avoiding the utilitarian attitude [towards the body] loses its *raison d'etre* and gives ground. But only to the extent that a person loved in this way — and this is most important — is equally ready to give herself or himself in love" (LR, pp. 181-183)

**5i.** According to "the law of the absorption of shame by love" (LR, p. 181), nakedness does not offend nor elicit shame in relationships in which the persons are "conscious of the gift" given and have "resolved to respond to it in an equally personal way." Instead, in this situation, the "human body in its nakedness [becomes] a sign of trust and ...the source of a particular interpersonal 'communication'" (224).

## 6. Lust and Concupiscence: "The Second Discovery of Sex"

Concupiscence refers to man's disordered passions. It comes from sin, inclines us to sin, but it is not a sin in itself. "Lust" is broader than the disorder of the sexual appetite, but most often refers to this.

- Lust is "un-inspired" sexual desire; sexual desire void of the love of God.
- With lust we encounter the basic principle that we cannot give what we do not have.
- Lust seeks "the sensation of sexuality" apart from a true communion of persons.
- Lust fails to respect the other as a subject created "for his/her own sake" and treats the other as an object to be used for my own selfish end.
- Lust shatters the original experiences of solitude, unity, and nakedness.

**6a.** "The human body in its masculinity / femininity has almost lost the capacity of expressing this love in which the man-person becomes a gift." We add the expression "almost" because "the nuptial meaning of the body has not been completely suffocated by concupiscence, only habitually threatened. The 'heart' has become a battlefield between love and lust. The more lust dominates the heart, the less the [heart] experiences the nuptial meaning of the body" (126).

**6b.** Lust "passes on the ruins of the matrimonial significance of the body and . . . aims directly . . . to satisfy only the sexual need of the body" (149).

**6c.** "Concupiscence, in itself, is not capable of promoting . . . the communion of persons. By itself, it does not unite, but appropriates. The relationship of the gift is changed into the relationship of appropriation" (127).

**6d.** Lust "is not always plain and obvious; sometimes it is concealed, so that it passes itself off as 'love.'. . . Does this mean that it is our duty to distrust the human heart? No! It only means that we must keep it under control" (126).

**6e.** "Liberation from lust" along with "the freedom of the gift" which it affords "is the condition of all life together in truth" (158-159).

## 7. Woman's Particular "Disability" and Man's Particular Responsibility

"To the woman [God] said, '. . . in pain you shall bring forth children, yet your desire shall be for your husband and he shall rule over you'" (Gn 3:16).

- The whole of human history has been marked by male domination.
- Woman's special genius (her "receptivity" to the gift) is now seen as a burden or even a curse.
- Throughout history, all that is feminine will be subject to a particular prejudice or even hatred (misogyny).
- If men tend to *use* women, women often will *allow themselves to be used.*

**7a.** The words of Genesis 3:16 "seem to refer to a particular 'disability' of woman as compared with man." As history attests, woman will feel a "form of inequality [manifested] as a lack of full unity precisely in the vast context of union with man, to which both were called [equally as persons] according to Genesis 2:24" (120)

**7b.** If lust and domination prevail "on the part of the man, the instincts that the woman directs towards him . . . can — and do — assume a similar character. And sometimes, perhaps, they precede the man's 'desire,' or even aim at arousing it and giving it impetus" (123).

**7c.** Both "the man and the woman have become . . . subject to lust. And therefore the lot of both is shame, which with its deep resonance touches the innermost recesses both of the male and female personality, although in a different way" (123).

**7d.** From "'the beginning' man was to have been the guardian of the reciprocity of donation and its true balance. . . . Although the maintenance of the balance of the gift seems to have been entrusted to both, a special responsibility rests with the man above all, as if it depended more on him whether this balance is maintained or broken, or even — if already broken — re-established" (128-129).

**7e.** "Adultery in the heart is committed not only because man 'looks' in this way at a woman who is not his wife, but *precisely* because he looks at a woman in this way. Even if he looked in this way at his wife, he could likewise commit adultery 'in his heart'" (157).

## 8. The Redemption of the Body

We "groan inwardly as we wait for . . . the redemption of our bodies" (Ro 8:23).

- For John Paul, the "redemption of the body" is not one aspect of redemption, but speaks of the reality of redemption in its entirety.
- We must accept the tension of "already, but-not-yet." In this life we will always be able to recognize a "system of forces" at war within us. Victory is gradual.
- St. Paul vividly describes the interior battle with concupiscence (see Ro 7). But he also speaks of the power of redemption at work within us which is able to do far more than we ever think or imagine (see Eph 3:20).
- Balancing these truths, we find both a real battle with lust and the possibility of a real victory over it.

**8a.** The "redemption of the body . . . is the redemption of man. At the same time [it is] the redemption of the world: it has a cosmic dimension" (299-300). "This is, in fact, the perspective of the whole Gospel, of the whole teaching, in fact of the whole mission of Christ" (175).

**8b.** The "'ethos of redemption' [is], more precisely, the ethos of the redemption of the body." This "is certainly a 'new' ethos . . . with regard to the state of 'historical' man." It is new "in a universal sense and significance." It is also new "in comparison with the Old Testament" (174).

**8c.** The "judgement expressed [in the Old Testament], regarding the body and sex, . . . is not concerned directly with putting some order in the heart of man, but with putting order in the entire social life, at the base of which stands, as always, marriage and the family" (137). In fact, "in the interpretation of the Old Testament, . . . the prohibition of adultery is balanced — you could say — by the compromise with bodily concupiscence" (136). Therefore, prescriptions of the Old Testament do not "reveal any tendency to change ethos in a fundamental way. . . . For such a transformation it is necessary to wait until the Sermon on the Mount" (144). Here we encounter "the possibility and the necessity of transforming what has been weighed down by the lust of the flesh" (170-171).

**8d.** "There were . . . under the regime of the Old Covenant, people who possessed the . . . grace of the Holy Spirit. . . . Conversely, there exist carnal men under the New Covenant, still distanced from the perfection of the New Law" (St. Thomas Aquinas, CCC, n. 1964).

**8e.** The "'redemption of the body' is expressed not only in the resurrection as victory over death. It is present also in Christ's words addressed to 'historical' man . . . when . . . Christ called man to overcome concupiscence, even in the uniquely interior movements of the human heart" (301).

NOTES

**8f.** The redemption of the body refers not only to our hope of final resurrection, but also to the "hope of every day" which "manifests its power in human works and even in the very movements of the human heart, clearing a path, in a certain sense, for the great eschatological hope bound with the redemption of the body" (301).

**8g.** "Someone, I was told, at the sight of a very beautiful body, felt impelled to glorify the Creator. The sight of it increased his love for God to the point of tears. Anyone who entertains such feelings in such circumstances is already risen . . . before the general resurrection" (John Climacus, *The Ladder of Divine Ascent*, 15th step, 58, p. 168).

**8h.** "Christ will raise us up 'on the last day'; but it is also true that, in a certain way, we have already risen with Christ. . . . Christian life is already now on earth a participation in the death and resurrection of Christ. . . . United with Christ by Baptism, believers already truly participate in the heavenly life of the risen Christ, but this life remains 'hidden with Christ in God'" (CCC, n. 1002-3).

**8i.** Since Christ's resurrection occurred in history, "*the 'redemption of the body' is already an aspect of human life on earth.* This redemption is not just an eschatological reality but a historical one as well. It shapes the history of the salvation of concrete living people, and, in a special way, of those people who in the sacrament of matrimony are called . . . to become 'one flesh' (Gn 2:24), in keeping with the intent of the Creator announced to the first parents before the fall" (PC, p. 326).

**8j.** "In the Sermon on the Mount, Christ does not invite man to return to the state of original innocence, because humanity has irrevocably left it behind, but He calls him to rediscover — on the foundation of the perennial and, so to speak, indestructible meanings of what is 'human' — the living forms of the 'new man.' In this way . . . a continuity is established between the 'beginning' and the perspective of redemption. In the ethos of the redemption of the body, the original ethos of creation will have to be taken up again" (175).

**8k.** Christ's words in the Sermon on the Mount "bear witness that the original power (therefore also the grace) of the mystery of creation has become for each of [us] power (that is, grace) of the mystery of redemption" (167).

**8l.** Historical man "should find again the dignity and holiness of the conjugal union 'in the body' on the basis of the mystery of redemption" (346).

## 9. Manichaeism: The Tenacious Heresy

If we are to understand the proper sense of Christ's words, we must contend with the "inveterate habits" which spring from Manichaeism in our way of thinking and evaluating things (see 165).

- This dualistic heresy arose in the 3rd century and has managed to infiltrate the thinking of numerous Christians to a greater or lesser degree ever since.
- Tragically, it seems many tenets of this heresy would pass themselves off as "sound Christian doctrine" if read from the typical American pulpit.
- How many people think the Church "negates the value of sex" or merely "tolerates" it because of the necessity of procreation? These are Manichaean attitudes (see 163)!

**9a.** "If taken with the seriousness it deserves, John Paul II's *Theology of the Body* may prove to be the decisive moment in exorcizing the Manichaean demon and its depreciation of human sexuality from Catholic moral theology" (WH, p. 342).

**9b.** Manichaeism sprang from dualism and "saw the source of evil in matter, in the body, and therefore proclaimed the condemnation of everything that is corporeal in man. And since corporeity is manifested in man mainly through sex, so the condemnation was extended to marriage and to conjugal life" (161).

**9c.** "The appropriate interpretation of Christ's words . . . must be absolutely free of Manichaean elements in thought and in attitude" (163). The "Manichaean way of understanding and evaluating man's body and sexuality is essentially alien to the Gospel. . . . Anyone who wants to see in [Christ's] words a Manichaean perspective would be committing an essential error" (165).

**9d.** "Whereas, for the Manichaean mentality, the body and sexuality constitute . . . an 'anti-value'; for Christianity, on the contrary, they always constitute a 'value not sufficiently appreciated'" (163-164).

**9e.** "Christ demands detachment from the evil of 'lust,' . . . but His enunciation does not let it be supposed in any way that the object of that desire, that is, the woman who is 'looked at lustfully,' is an evil." Such a notion "would mean a certain acceptance — perhaps not fully conscious — of the Manichaean 'anti-value.' It would not constitute a real and deep victory over the evil of the act [of lust]...; on the contrary, there would be concealed in it the great danger of justifying the act [of lust] to the detriment of the object (the essential error of Manichaean ethos consists, in fact, just in this)" (164).

**9f.** We can see that the Manichaean condemnation of the body and sex "might — and may always be — a loophole to avoid the requirements set in the Gospel" (162).

## 10. The Interpretation of Suspicion

Redemption does not magically remove the consequences of sin during our historical existence (we still suffer, get ill, grow old, struggle with weaknesses and the pull of concupiscence, etc. [see CCC, nn. 978, 1226, 1264, 1426]). Yet, the reality of concupiscence must not cause us to hold the human heart in continual suspicion.

- A "master of suspicion" is a person who does not know or does not fully believe in the transforming power of the Gospel.
- Lust holds sway in his own heart so he projects the same onto everyone else.
- In his mind the human body will always rouse concupiscence; it can do nothing else.
- We must be careful not to fall into the trap of "holding the form of religion" while "denying the power of it" (2 Tm 3:5).

**10a.** "Man cannot stop at putting the 'heart' in a state of continual and irreversible suspicion due to the manifestations of the lust of the flesh. . . . Redemption is a truth, a reality, in the name of which man must feel called, and called with efficacy" (167).

**10b.** When "the human heart is bound in permanent suspicion" man is unable to tap into his "deepest and yet most real possibilities." He is unable to give voice to "the innermost layers of his potentiality. . . . The ethos of redemption, on the other hand, is based on a close alliance with those layers" (176).

**10c.** "The meaning of life is the antithesis of the interpretation 'of suspicion.' This interpretation is very different, it is radically different from what we discover in Christ's words in the Sermon on the Mount. These words reveal . . . another vision of man's possibilities" (168).

**10d.** What "are the 'concrete possibilities of man'? And of which man are we speaking? Of man *dominated* by lust or of man *redeemed by Christ*? This is what is at stake: the *reality* of Christ's redemption. *Christ has redeemed us!* This means He has given us the possibility of realizing the *entire truth* of our being; He has set our freedom free from the *domination* of concupiscence. And if redeemed man still sins, this is not due to an imperfection of Christ's redemptive act, but to man's will not to avail himself of the grace which flows from that act" (VS, n. 103).

## 11. Eros, Ethos and Spontaneity

Do Christ's words in the Sermon on the Mount condemn the erotic? Do they hinder the spontaneity of erotic love?

- Most people think of Christ's words only as a prohibition without seeing "the really deep and essential values that this prohibition ensures" (171).
- Christ not only wants to protect these values. He wants to make them accessible to us if we would but learn to open our hearts to them (see 171).

**11a.** In "the erotic sphere, 'eros' and 'ethos' do not differ from each other, [they] are not opposed to each other." Instead, eros and ethos "are called to meet in the human heart, and, in this meeting, to bear fruit" (171).

**11b.** "It is necessary continually to rediscover in what is 'erotic' the nuptial meaning of the body and the true dignity of the gift. This is the role of the human spirit. . . . If it does not assume this role, the very attraction of the senses and the passion of the body may stop at mere lust, devoid of ethical value." If man stops here, he "does not experience that fullness of 'eros' — which means the aspiration of the human spirit towards the true, good, and beautiful — so that what is 'erotic' also becomes true, good, and beautiful" (171).

**11c.** "It is very often thought that it is ethos itself that takes away spontaneity from what is erotic in man's life and behavior. . . . But this opinion is erroneous and, in any case, superficial. Obstinately accepting it and upholding it, we will never reach the full dimensions of eros" (172).

**11d.** The law of the Gospel "inclines us to act spontaneously by the prompting of charity" (CCC, n. 1972).

**11e.** Whoever accepts Christ's words about lust, "must know that he is also *called to a full and mature spontaneity* of the relations that spring from the perennial attraction of masculinity and femininity. This very spontaneity is the gradual fruit of the discernment of the impulses of one's own heart" (172).

**11f.** [Paraphrasing] We must learn with perseverance and consistency the meaning of our bodies, the meaning of our sexuality. We must learn this not only in the abstract (although this, too, is necessary), but above all in the interior reactions of our own "hearts." This is a "science" which cannot really be learned only from books, because it is a question here of deep knowledge of our interior life. Deep in the heart we learn to distinguish between what, on the one hand, composes the great riches of sexuality and sexual attraction, and what, on the other hand, bears only the sign of lust. And although these internal movements of the heart can sometimes be confused with one another, we have been called by Christ to acquire a mature and complete evaluation. "And it should be added that this task *can* be carried out and is really worthy of man" (172).

## 12. Life According to the Flesh/Spirit and Justification by Faith

Walk "by the Spirit, and do not gratify the desires of the flesh. For the desires of the flesh are against the Spirit, and the desires of the Spirit are against the flesh" (Gal 5:16-17).

- This *does not* mean that the spirit is good and the body is "bad" (recall the *Catechism*'s "ode to the flesh" [n. 1015])!
- The "flesh" is the whole person (body and soul) cut off from God's inspiration.

- Living "according to the Spirit" refers to the man who lives a re-integrated life (of soul and body) by the power of the Holy Spirit dwelling in his body.
- Those who live according to the Spirit are "justified by faith."

**12a.** "It is not a question here only of the body (matter) and of the spirit (soul)." These "constitute from the beginning the very essence of man" (191).

**12b.** "From the context it is clear that for the Apostle it is not a question of discriminating against and condemning the body, which with the spiritual soul constitutes man's nature and personal subjectivity" (DV, n. 55).

**12c.** "Anyone who . . . lives 'according to the flesh'...ceases to be suitable for the real gift of himself . . . which is organically connected with the nuptial meaning of the human body" (198).

**12d.** It is "those powers of the Spirit which bring about 'justification,' that is, which enable justice 'to abound' in man . . . to the extent that God Himself willed and which He expects" (194).

**12e.** Justification by faith refers to "the power of Christ Himself operating within man by means of the Holy Spirit." It "is not just a dimension of the divine plan of man's salvation . . . but is . . . a real power that operates in man and is revealed . . . in his actions" (192,193).

**12f.** "As much as 'concupiscence' darkens the horizon of the inward vision and deprives the heart of the clarity of desires and aspirations, so much does 'life according to the Spirit' . . . permit man and woman to find again the true liberty of the gift, united to the awareness of the spousal meaning of the body in its masculinity and femininity" (349).

## 13. Purity of Heart

"Blessed are the pure in heart, for they shall see God" (Mt 5:8). "To the pure all things are pure, but to the corrupt and unbelieving nothing is pure" (Ti 1:15).

- Christian purity is not prudishness or puritanism!
- Authentic purity recognizes that those parts of the body that fallen men think are "less honorable" actually deserve "all the greater honor" (1 Co 12:23).
- Purity has a moral dimension as a virtue, but it also has a charismatic dimension as a gift of the Holy Spirit
- Purity is connected with piety which is respect for the work of God. Unchastity is a violation of piety because the body is a temple of the Holy Spirit (1Co 6:19).

**13a.** "Purity is the glory of the human body before God. It is God's glory in the human body, through which masculinity and femininity are manifested" (209).

**13b.** "Even now [purity of heart] enables us to see *according to* God...; it lets us perceive the human body — ours and our neighbor's — as a temple of the Holy Spirit, a manifestation of divine beauty" (CCC, n. 2519).

**13c.** Man must learn "to be the true master of his own deep impulses, like a guardian who watches over a hidden spring; and finally to draw form those impulses what is fitting for 'purity of heart'" (172).

**13d.** Purity "is not just abstention from unchastity or temperance." There is "another role of the virtue of purity . . . which is, it could be said, more positive than negative." The positive dimension of purity "opens the way to a more and more perfect discovery of the dignity of the human body" (200, 213).

**13e.** "In mature purity, man enjoys the fruits of the victory won over lust, a victory of which St. Paul writes, exhorting man to 'control his own body in holiness and honor' (1 Thes 4:4)." He enjoys the "efficacy of the gift of the Holy Spirit" who restores to his experience of the body "all its simplicity, its explicitness, and also its interior joy" (213).

**13f.** "Purity is a requirement of love. It is the dimension of its interior truth in man's 'heart'" (177).

## 14. The Freedom for Which Christ Has Set Us Free

"For freedom Christ has set us free; stand fast therefore, and do not submit again to a yoke of slavery. . . . For you were called to freedom, brethren; only do not use your freedom as an opportunity for the flesh, but through love be servants of one another" (Gal 5:1, 13).

- We know true purity only to the degree that we are "free with the freedom for which Christ set us free" (see 197).
- According to St. Paul, the freedom necessary for love also provides the opportunity to indulge "the flesh."
- We must not remove the freedom we have to sin! For in the same stroke we eradicate the freedom that is necessary to love.
- If we must chain ourselves to avoid sin, we are not free, we are *in chains*.
- If we are not free in this sense, we have yet to pass over from the Old to the New law.
- True freedom is liberation not from the *external* "constraint" that calls me to good, but from the *internal* constraint that hinders my choice of the good.

**14a.** The "dimension of the new Gospel ethos is nothing but an appeal to human freedom, an appeal to its fuller implementation and, in a way, to fuller 'utilization' of the potential of the human spirit" (197).

**14b.** The man who indulges lust "ceases to be capable of that freedom for which 'Christ set us free.'" This is the "antithesis" and the "negation" of freedom (198).

**14c.** The very manner in which we conceive marriage (and the relationship of the sexes in general) "must be from the start, to the greatest extent possible, freed from purely impulse-oriented, naturalistic presuppositions and shaped personalistically" (PC, p. 330). In this impulse-oriented view "there seems to be a tendency to limit the possibility of virtue and magnify the 'necessity of sin' in [the sexual] sphere. Personalism, with its emphasis on self-determination, would entail the opposite tendency." It "would perceive the possibility of virtue, based on self-control and sublimation" (PC, p. 286).

**14d.** "Man must feel called to rediscover, nay more, to realize the nuptial meaning of the body and to express in this way the interior freedom of the gift [through] that spiritual state and that spiritual power which are derived from mastery of the lust of the flesh" (167).

## 15. Portraying the Naked Body in Art

Can the naked body be portrayed in art without offending its dignity?

- Appropriate portrayals of the body help us "overcome the limits of shame" (see 222)

- Inappropriate portrayals of the body "overstep the limits of shame" (see 223).
- Pornography and appropriate art is distinguished by the intention of the "artist."
- We can say that the problem with pornography is not that it shows too much of the person, but that it shows far too little.

**15a.** "The man of developed sensitivity overcomes . . . the limits of that shame," yet "only with difficulty and interior resistence" (222).

**15b.** The portrayal of the naked body in art raises a "very delicate problem" (221) since "that 'element of the gift' is, so to speak, suspended in the dimension of an unknown reception and an unforseen response, and thereby it is in a way 'threatened' . . . in the sense that it may become an anonymous object of . . . abuse" (225). This "does not mean that the human body, in its nakedness, cannot become a subject of works of art — but only that this problem is not purely aesthetic, nor morally indifferent" (221). It is "connected with a special responsibility" (227).

**15c.** There "are works of art whose subject is the human body in its nakedness" which help us see "the whole personal mystery of man. In contact with these works . . . we learn in a way that nuptial meaning of the body which corresponds to, and is the measure of, 'purity of heart.' But there are also works of art . . . which arouse objection . . . — not because of their object, since the human body in itself always has its inalienable dignity — but because of the quality or way of its reproduction, portrayal, artistic representation" (227-228).

**15d.** "It seems that Michelangelo, in his own way, allowed himself to be guided by the evocative words of the Book of Genesis which . . . reveals: 'The man and his wife were both naked, yet felt no shame (Gn 2:25). *The Sistine Chapel* is . . . *the sanctuary of the theology of the human body*." For "in the context of the light that comes from God, the human body also keeps its splendor and its dignity. If it is removed from this dimension, it becomes in some way an object, which depreciates very easily, since only before the eyes of God can the human body remain naked and unclothed, and keep its splendor and beauty intact" (*L'Osservatore Romano*, April 13, 1994).

# Cycle 3: Eschatological Man

(TB, pp. 233-261)

A "total vision of man" must also look towards man's ultimate destiny. Only in this light do our origin and our history take on their meaning. In these 9 general audience addresses delivered between November 11, 1981 and February 10, 1982, John Paul weds his Carmelite mysticism with his phenomenological insights for a vision of the eschaton never before articulated. He reflects upon the body and sexuality as we will experience them in the resurrection when all things will be consummated in Christ Jesus. This is the third and final element in the "triptych" that makes up John Paul's "adequate anthropology."

## 1. The Resurrection of the Body

"I believe in the resurrection of the body and the life everlasting. Amen" (Apostle's Creed).

- Many people have an erroneous "super-spiritual" view of heaven.
- They tend to see the body as a shell and they're anxious to get rid of it.
- Our bodies will certainly be different (recall that the disciples didn't readily recognize Jesus in His risen body), but in the final reality, we will still be body-persons.

**1a.** "'On no point does the Christian faith meet with more opposition than on the resurrection of the body.' It is very commonly accepted that the life of the human person continues in a spiritual fashion after death. But how can we believe that this body, so clearly mortal, could rise to everlasting life" (CCC, n. 996)?

**1b.** "The resurrection is the reply of the God of life to the historical inevitability of death" (250). "The resurrection constitutes the definitive accomplishment of the redemption of the body" (252).

**1c.** The truth about man's destiny "cannot be understood as a state of the soul alone, separated (according to Plato: liberated) from the body." It "must be understood as the state of man definitively and perfectly 'integrated' through [the perfect] union of the soul and the body" (240).

**1d.** "A soul without a body is exactly the opposite of what Plato thought it is. It is not free but bound. It is in an extreme form of paralysis." The human soul *needs* the body to express itself — not only on earth but in heaven as well. "That is why the resurrection of the body is . . . not a dispensable extra. When death separates the two we have a freak, a monster, an obscenity. That is why we are terrified of ghosts and corpses, though both are harmless: they are the obscenely separated aspects of what belongs together as one. That is why Jesus wept at Lazarus' grave: not merely for His bereavement but for this cosmic obscenity" (Peter Kreeft, *Everything You Ever Wanted to Know about Heaven* [Ignatius Press, 1990], p. 93)

## 2. Christ Points us to the Future

"For in the resurrection they neither marry nor are given in marriage" (Mt 22:30).

- Christ's words may seem to undermine all we've said about the greatness of marriage.
- In fact, Christ's words point to the crowning glory of all we've said.
- Marriage exists "from the beginning" to point us to the "Marriage of the Lamb" (Rev 19:7).
- In the eschaton, the primordial sacrament will give way to the divine prototype.
- This means that the union of the sexes is not man's end-all-and-be-all. It is only an "icon." We must be very careful never to treat it as an "idol."

**2a.** "As can be seen from [Christ's] words, marriage, that union in which . . . 'they become one flesh' (Gn 2:24) . . . belongs exclusively to this age." Yet it is very significant that "Christ reveals the new condition of the human body in the resurrection . . . precisely by proposing a reference and a comparison with the condition in which man had participated since the 'beginning'" (238, 239).

**2b.** "Marriage and procreation in itself did not determine definitively the original and fundamental meaning of being a body, or of being, as a body, male and female. Marriage and procreation merely give a concrete reality to that meaning in the dimension of history" (247)

**2c.** The "need to give oneself to and unite with another person . . . is not finally and completely satisfied simply by union with another human being. Considered in the perspective of the person's eternal existence, marriage is only a tentative solution of the problem of a union of persons through love." Celibacy for the kingdom, "in the perspective of eternal life, is another attempt to solve the problem" (LR, pp. 253-54).

## 3. Reflecting on the "Eschatological Experience"?

How can we possibly talk about subjective experience in relation to the final resurrection when we have no experience of it whatsoever?

- Christ calls historical man to look in two directions — the beginning and the future.
- There is a clear and important distinction and "discontinuity" between our original, historical, and eschatological existence. But there is also a continuity.

**3a.** "When Christ speaks of the future resurrection, His words do not fall in a void. The experience of mankind, and especially the experience of the body, enable the listener to unite with those words the image of his new existence in the 'future world,' for which earthly experience supplies the substratum and the base." Therefore, an "adequate theological reconstruction is possible" (246).

**3b.** If we are to penetrate "into the very essence of what will be the beatific vision," it is "necessary to let oneself be guided by that 'range of experience' of truth and love which goes beyond the limits of the cognitive and spiritual possibilities of man in temporality" (242).

**3c.** Of course, the resurrection "will be a completely new experience." Yet "at the same time it will not be alienated in any way from what man took part in from 'the beginning' nor from what, in the historical dimension of his existence, constituted in him the source of the tension between spirit and body, concerning mainly the procreative meaning of the body and sex" (248).

## 4. The Spiritualization of the Body

"For when they rise from the dead, they . . . are like angels in heaven" (Mk 12:25). "It is sown a physical body, it is raised a spiritual body" (1 Co 15:44).

- Jesus says we will be *like* angels. He doesn't say we will be angels.
- The "spiritualization of the body" refers to the perfect integration of body and soul.
- We can achieve a mature level of integration in this life, but the possibility of opposition between body and soul remains.
- In the eschaton the "war within" is completely eliminated.

**4a.** "It is obvious that it is not a question here of transforming man's nature into that of the angels, that is, a purely spiritual one. . . . If it were . . . it would be meaningless to speak of the resurrection" (239).

**4b.** St. Paul "insists on the fact that body and soul are capable of being . . . spiritual" (261).

**4c.** Spiritualization means that "the forces of the spirit will permeate the energies of the body." Because of man's very nature, "perfection cannot exist in a mutual opposition of spirit and body, but in a deep harmony between them, in safeguarding the primacy of the spirit" (241).

**4d.** "Pre-Cartesian cultures did not divide reality into two mutually exclusive categories of purely immaterial spirit and purely nonspiritual matter. Rather, they saw all matter as in-formed, in-breathed by spirit. . . . Descartes initiates 'angelism' when he says, 'My whole essence is in thought alone.' Matter and spirit now become 'two clear and distinct ideas.' . . . This is *our* common sense; we have inherited these categories, like nonremovable contact lenses, from Descartes, and it is impossible for us to understand pre-Cartesian thinkers while we wear them. Thus we are constantly reading our modern categories . . . into the authors of the Bible" (Peter Kreeft, *Everything You Ever Wanted to Know about Heaven*, pp. 86-87)

## 5. The Divinization of the Body

We are called to "participate in the divine nature" (2 Pt 1:4).

- The "spiritualization" of man refers to the perfect indwelling of the divine Person of the Holy Spirit.
- Hence, man's heavenly "spiritualization" has its source in his "divinization."

**5a.** For "'eschatological' man . . . the degree of his 'divinization' [is] incomparably superior to the one that can be attained in earthly life. It . . . is a question not only of a different degree, but, in a way, of another kind of 'divinization'" (242).

**5b.** In the resurrection, "penetration and permeation of what is essentially human by what is essentially divine, will then reach its peak so that the life of the human spirit will arrive at such fullness which previously had been absolutely inaccessible to it." God will communicate "His very divinity not only to man's soul, but to his whole psychosomatic subjectivity" (242).

## 6. The Beatific Vision

"For now we see in a mirror dimly, but then face to face" (1 Co 13:12).

- The beatific vision was foreshadowed (dimly, of course) right from the beginning in the experience of original happiness.
- Recall that original happiness was revealed through the experience of original unity and nakedness. It was man and woman's experience of love and communion with God and with one another.
- The beatific vision is the definitive fulfillment of every human longing for union.
- The beatific vision is man's perfect participation in grace.
- In a word, that mystery we shall behold "face to face" is love (see 1 Jn 4:8) . And love is gift; and gift is grace; and grace received is communion — *with the divine.*

**6a.** The object of the beatific vision "will be that mystery hidden in the Father from eternity, a mystery which in time was revealed in Christ, in order to be accomplished incessantly through the Holy Spirit" (243).

**6b.** The beatific vision is "a concentration of knowledge and love on God Himself." This knowledge "cannot be other than full participation in the interior life of God, that is, in the very trinitarian reality" (244).

**6c.** Man "can fully discover his true self only in a sincere giving of himself" (GS, n. 24).

**6d.** The absence of marriage in heaven "is explained not only with the end of history, but also — and above all — with [man's] response to that 'self communication' of the divine Subject." In the beatific vision, "the gift of Himself on God's part . . . is absolutely superior to any experience proper to earthly life. The reciprocal gift of oneself to God . . . will be the response of God's gift of Himself to man." For man, this mutual exchange "will become completely and definitively beatifying" (244).

**6e.** The "gift [God makes] to man . . . in Christ is a 'total' . . . gift." This "is indicated precisely by the analogy of spousal love." Yet "as a creature [man] is not capable of 'receiving' the gift of God in the transcendental fullness of His divinity. Such a 'total gift' (uncreated) is shared only by God Himself in the 'triune communion of the Persons.'" Man receives "in a certain sense 'all' that God 'could' give of Himself to man considering the limited faculties of man [as a] creature" (331).

**6f.** The beatific vision is a "union with God in His Trinitarian mystery and of intimacy with Him in the perfect communion of persons." This divine-human communion "will be nourished by the vision, 'face to face' . . . of that more perfect communion — because it is purely divine — which is the trinitarian communion of the divine Persons" (243).

## 7. The Definitive Fulfillment of the Nuptial Meaning of the Body

The words of Genesis 2:24 refer "especially to this world," but "not completely" (249). These are "the words that constitute the sacrament of marriage" (76). Hence, like all sacraments, the "one flesh" unity of marriage points in some way to the "other world."

- John Paul states several times that we will be raised as male and female.
- Maleness and femaleness will remain an integral part of our communion in heaven, even if experienced in an entirely new dimension.
- Sexual difference and our longing for union reveal that we are created for eternal communion with *the* Eternal Communion: Father, Son, and Holy Spirit.
- The nuptial meaning of the body will be fulfilled in an eternal dimension of "incarnate communion" inclusive of all who respond to the wedding invitation of the Lamb.

**7a.** The heavenly reality "will be above all man's rediscover of himself, not only in the depths of his own person [fulfillment of original solitude], but also in that union which is proper to the world of [human] persons in their psychosomatic constitution [fulfillment of original unity]" (244).

**7b.** In "the resurrection, we discover — in an eschatological dimension — the same characteristics that qualified the 'nuptial' meaning of the body." This time, however, all those characteristics are fulfilled "in the meeting with the mystery of the living God, which is revealed through the vision of Him 'face to face'" (243).

**7c.** The "'nuptial' meaning of the body in the resurrection to the future life will correspond perfectly both to the fact that man, as male and female, is a person created 'in the image and likeness of God,' and to the fact that this image is realized in the communion of persons. That 'nuptial' meaning of being a body will be realized, therefore, as a meaning that is perfectly personal and communitarian at the same time" (247).

**7d.** The "virginal state of the body will be totally manifested as the eschatological fulfillment of the 'nuptial' meaning of the body" (244).

**7e.** Heaven will be the experience "of perpetual 'virginity' (united to the nuptial meaning of the body) and of the perpetual 'intersubjectivity' of all men, who will become (as males and females) sharers in the resurrection" (254).

**7f.** "That perennial meaning of the human body — to which the existence of every man, weighed down by the heritage of concupiscence, has necessarily brought a series of limitations, struggles, and sufferings — will then be revealed again in such simplicity and splendor when every participant in the 'other world' will find again in his glorified body the source of the freedom of the gift" (248).

**7g.** "In the joys of their love [God gives spouses] here on earth a foretaste of the wedding feast of the Lamb" (CCC, n. 1642).

**7h.** The Church "longs to be united with Christ, her Bridegroom, in the glory of heaven" where she "will rejoice one day with [her] Beloved, in a happiness and rapture that can never end" (CCC, n. 1821).

## 8. The Communion of Saints

For man, the heavenly communion of saints is the ultimate and definitive "*communio personarum*." It is the unity in "one body" of all who respond to the wedding invitation of the Lamb.

- The spousal analogy ultimately breaks down, but we use it to make a theological "approximation" of the heavenly mystery of communion.
- The communion of saints is a multitude of created communions consolidated in communion with each other by their eternal vision of the Uncreated Communion.

- It is the perfect experience of "unity-in-distinction" or "unity-in-plurality."
- In this "union of communion" (244), we will see all and be seen by all. We will know all and be known by all. And God will be "all in all" (Eph 1:23).

**8a.** "The concentration of knowledge and love on God Himself in the trinitarian communion of Persons can find a beatifying response in [man] only through realizing mutual communion adapted to created persons. And for this reason we profess faith in the communion of saints" (244).

**8b.** "*For man*, this consummation will be the final realization of the unity of the human race, which God willed from creation. . . . Those who are united with Christ will form the community of the redeemed, 'the holy city' of God, 'the Bride, the wife of the Lamb'" (CCC, n. 1045).

**8c.** The "source of the freedom of the gift . . . will nourish also with that gift each of the communions which will make up the great community of the communion of saints" (248).

**8d.** "We must think of the reality of the 'other world' in the categories of the rediscovery of a new, perfect subjectivity of everyone, and at same time of the rediscovery of a new, perfect intersubjectivity of all." This "reality signifies the real and definitive fulfillment of human subjectivity, and . . . the definitive fulfillment of the 'nuptial' meaning of the body." In "this way eschatological reality will become the source of the perfect realization of the 'trinitarian order' in the created world of persons" (245).

## 9. The First and the Last Adam

"'The first man, Adam, became a living being'; the last Adam became a life-giving spirit. . . . As we have borne the image of the man of earth, so we will bear the image of the man of heaven" (1 Co 15:45, 49).

- St. Paul unites eschatological man with original man and speaks of the weakness of historical man ("What is sown in weakness is raised in power," v. 43)
- Historical man lives in a "tension between the two poles" of the first and last Adam.
- This tension awakens a great hope, akin to a woman's labor pains (see Ro 8:23).
- The body is in "bondage to decay" (Ro 8:21). It is destined to "return to dust" (Gn 3:19), but also to be re-quickened by the life-giving spirit ("breath") of the last Adam.

**9a.** The resurrection is not merely "a return to the state which the soul enjoyed before sin." That would not "correspond to the internal logic of the whole economy of salvation, to the most profound meaning of the *mystery* of the redemption." The resurrection "can only be an *introduction* to a *new fullness* . . . that presupposes the whole of human history, formed by the drama of the tree of the knowledge of good and evil" (255-256).

**9b.** "The humanity of the 'first Adam,' the 'man of earth,' bears in itself . . . a particular potential (which is capacity and readiness) to receive all that became the 'second Adam,' the 'man of heaven,' namely, . . . what [Christ] became in His resurrection" (253).

**9c.** Every man experiences "the interior desire for glory" because "every man bears in himself the image of Adam [who] is also called to bear in himself the image of Christ, the image of the risen One" (253, 254).

**9d.** Christ "fully reveals man to himself and makes his supreme calling clear" (GS, n. 22).

# PART II

## How Are We To Live?

## *Applying an Adequate Anthropology*

N O T E S

# Cycle 4: Celibacy for the Kingdom

(TB, pp. 262-303)

This cycle marks a shift from the development of an "adequate anthropology" to its application. In these 14 general audience addresses delivered between March 10, 1982 and July 21, 1982, John Paul applies his "total vision of man" to the vocation of celibacy "for the kingdom." It is significant that he treats celibacy *before* he discusses the sacramentality of marriage. For only in light of the celibate vocation does the marriage vocation take on its full meaning.

"Christian revelation recognizes two specific ways of realizing the vocation of the human person, in its entirety, to love: marriage and virginity or celibacy. Either one is in its own proper form an actuation of the most profound truth about man, of his being 'created in the image of God'" (FC, n. 11).

## 1. Eunuchs "For the Kingdom"

"For there are eunuchs who have been so from birth, and there are eunuchs who have been made eunuchs by men, and there are eunuchs who have made themselves eunuchs for the sake of the kingdom of heaven" (Mt 19:12).

- A eunuch is someone physically incapable of sexual relations.
- A eunuch "for the kingdom" is someone who freely forgoes sexual relations as a sign of that state in which men and women "neither marry nor are given in marriage."
- Those who are celibate for the kingdom "skip" the sacrament in anticipation of the ultimate reality, the "Marriage of the Lamb."
- By doing so they step outside the dimensions of history — while living within the dimensions of history — and proclaim to the world that "the kingdom of God is here."
- Although celibacy points us to "the kingdom," it is significant that Christ spoke of it not in His discussion with the Sadducees (Mt 22), but with the Pharisees (Mt 19).

**1a.** Earthly continence for the kingdom "is a sign that the body, whose end is not the grave, is directed to glorification. Already by this very fact . . . continence 'for the kingdom of heaven' is a witness among men that anticipates the future resurrection" (267).

**1b.** Christ's "words do not express a command by which all are bound, but a counsel which concerns only some persons" (263). Celibacy for the kingdom is "a kind of exception to what is rather a general rule of this life" (264).

**1c.** Christ's words "clearly indicate the importance of the personal choice and also the . . . particular grace" of this vocation (263). They indicate celibacy's "voluntary and supernatural character" (265).

**1d.** In the Jewish tradition marriage "had acquired a consecrated significance because of the promise made to Abraham by the Lord. . . . In this environment Christ's words determine a decisive turning point" (265, 266).

**1e.** "I know that what I am going to say to you now will cause great difficulty in your conscience, in your way of understanding the significance of the body. In fact, I shall speak to you of continence, and, undoubtedly, you will associate this with the state of physical deficiency, whether congenital or brought about by human cause. But I wish to tell you that continence can also be voluntary and chosen by man 'for the sake of the kingdom'" (266).

**1f.** In "order to clarify what the kingdom of heaven is for those who choose voluntary continence for the sake of it, the revelation of the nuptial relationship of Christ with the Church has a particular significance" (280).

## 2. Remaining in "Solitude" before God

In some way the celibate person freely chooses to remain in the "ache" of solitude before God in order to devote all of his longings for communion towards Christ and the Church.

- If it is "not good for man to be alone," Christian celibacy reveals that the ultimate fulfillment of solitude is found only in the "Marriage of the Lamb."
- Christian celibacy emphasizes that man is called to be a "Partner of the Absolute."

**2a.** Celibacy for the Kingdom "must demonstrate that man, in his deepest being, is . . . 'alone' before God, with God. Nevertheless, . . . what is an invitation to solitude for God in the call to continence for the kingdom of heaven at the same time respects both the 'dual nature of mankind' (that is, his masculinity and femininity) and the dimension of communion . . . that is proper to the person" (273).

**2b.** Even "though it is possible to conceive man as solitary before God, however, God Himself draws him from this 'solitude' when He [creates] 'a helper fit for him'" (272). Thus, the continent person "is capable of discovering in his solitude . . . a new and even fuller form of intersubjective communion with others" (273).

**2c.** "If Christ . . . speaks of 'making oneself' a eunuch, . . . He does not . . . seek to conceal the anguish that such a decision and its enduring consequences can have for a man for the normal (and on the other hand noble) inclinations of his nature" (272). Celibacy demands a "breaking away" from the good of marriage "connected with a certain self-sacrifice. That break also becomes the beginning of successive self-sacrifices that are indispensable if the first and fundamental choice [is to] be consistent in the breadth of one's entire earthly life" (274).

## 3. Celibacy Flows from the Redemption of the Body

The difference between marriage and celibacy must *never* be understood as the difference between a "legitimate" outlet for concupiscence on the one hand and repressing concupiscence on the other.

- *Everyone* is called by Christ to overcome the domination of concupiscence through the redemption of the body.
- Only upon experiencing a true level of freedom from concupiscence does the ethos of the Christian vocations (celibacy *and* marriage) make sense.
- *Both* flow from the same experience of the redemption of sexual desire.

- This is why celibacy is not only a matter of formation but of *transformation* (see 286).
- Without this redemption (this freedom), choosing celibacy for one's entire life is absurd. With it, not only does it become possible. It becomes quite attractive.

**3a.** Behind Christ's words about lust and about celibacy "are found the same anthropology and the same ethos." In fact, in "the invitation to voluntary continence . . . , the prospects of this ethos are enlarged upon" (274).

**3b.** "He who consciously chooses such continence, chooses, in a certain sense, a special participation in the mystery of the redemption (of the body)" (271).

**3c.** Concupiscence remains in the person "who must take the decision about continence 'for the kingdom of heaven.' He must put this decision into effect, subjugating the sinfulness of his [fallen] nature to the forces that spring from the mystery of the redemption of the body. He must do so just as any other man does . . . whose way remains that of matrimony. The only difference is the type of responsibility for the good chosen, just as the type of good chosen is different" (275).

**3d.** "At the basis of Christ's call to continence there is . . . the consciousness of the freedom of the gift, which is organically connected with the profound and mature knowledge of the nuptial meaning of the body" (283).

## 4. Doesn't St. Paul "Allow" Concupiscence in Marriage?

It "is well for them to remain single as I do. But if they cannot exercise self-control, they should marry. For it is better to marry than to be aflame with passion" (1 Co 7:9).

- Is marriage only intended for those who "can't handle" celibacy?
- This passage cannot be interpreted in isolation from Christ's words about lust.
- Indulging concupiscence would also be a blatant contradiction of Ephesians 5 and the whole New Testament ethos concerning marriage.

**4a.** "If it is true that marriage may also be a *remedium concupiscentiae* (see St. Paul: 'It is better to marry than to burn' — 1 Co 7:9) then this must be understood in the integral sense given it by the Christian Scriptures, which also teach of the 'redemption of the body' (Ro 8:23) and point to the sacrament of matrimony as a way of realizing this redemption" (PC, p. 327).

**4b.** St. Paul "expresses in his striking and at the same time paradoxical words, simply the thought that marriage is assigned to the spouses as an ethos. In the Pauline words, . . . the verb *ardere* [to be aflame] signifies a disorder of the passions, deriving from the concupiscence of the flesh. . . . 'Marriage,' however signifies the ethical order, which is consciously introduced in this context" (348).

## 5. Does St. Paul Devalue Marriage?

"It is well for a man not to touch a woman" (1 Co 7:1). "I wish that all were [celibate] as I myself am" (v. 7). "Do not seek marriage" (v. 27). Spouses will have "troubles in the flesh, and I would want to spare you that" (v. 28).

- John Paul asks if St. Paul might have a "personal aversion" to marriage, but concludes that a thoughtful reading of the text leads to another conclusion.

- The Pope insists that there is no reason to see symptoms of Manichaeism in Paul's teaching.
- Many suggest that Paul's perspective on marriage reflects a belief that Christ's return was imminent.

**5a.** Saint Paul interprets Christ's teaching about continence and marriage in a "style of this problem [that] is totally his own" (288). He interprets these vocations "in that very pastoral way that is proper to him, not sparing . . . entirely personal accents" (298).

**5b.** In St. Paul's "realistic observation" about marriage and the troubles it brings "we must see a just warning for those who — as at times young people do — hold that conjugal union and living together must bring them only happiness and joy. The experience of life shows that spouses are not rarely disappointed in what they were greatly expecting." If by Paul's warnings about marriage "he intends to say that true conjugal love — precisely that love by virtue of which '...the two become one flesh' (Gn 2:24) — is also a difficult love, he certainly remains on the grounds of evangelical truth" (290).

## 6. The "Superiority" of Celibacy

He "who marries . . . does well; and he who refrains from marriage will do better" (1 Co 7:38). "But each has his own special gift from God, one of one kind and one of another" (1 Co 7:7).

- Many have thought that if "celibacy is so good" marriage must be "so bad."
- Or, if religious celibacy is the state of "perfection," marriage must be the state of "imperfection." This is *absolutely not* the mind of the Church!
- Celibacy is "exceptional" because marriage remains the normal calling in this life.
- It is "better" in the sense that heavenly "marriage" is better than earthly marriage.
- One must carefully and prayerfully discern which "gift" he or she has been given.

**6a.** "The 'superiority' of continence to matrimony in the authentic Tradition of the Church never means disparagement of marriage or belittlement of its essential value. It does not . . . mean a shift, even implicit, on the Manichean positions, or a support of ways of evaluating or acting based on the Manichean understanding of the body and sexuality, matrimony and procreation." In Christ's words "we do not find any basis whatever for any disparagement of matrimony" (275).

**6b.** In Christ words about continence "there is no reference to the 'inferiority' of marriage with regard to the 'body,' or in other words with regard to the essence of marriage, consisting in the fact that man and woman join together in marriage, thus becoming 'one flesh.' . . . Christ's words on this point are quite clear." Christ proposes continence not "with prejudice against conjugal 'union of the body,' but only 'for the sake of the kingdom of heaven'" (276).

**6c.** Marriage and celibacy do not "divide the human (and Christian) community into two camps [as if there were] those who are 'perfect' because of continence and those who are 'imperfect' or 'less perfect' because of the reality of married life" (276).

**6d.** "Perfection of the Christian life . . . is measured with the rule of charity." This means that "perfection is possible and accessible to every man, both in a 'religious institute,' and in the 'world.'" In fact, a person who does not live in "the state of perfection" can nonetheless "reach a superior degree of perfection — whose measure is charity — in comparison to the person who does live in the 'state of perfection' with a lesser degree of charity" (277).

**6e.** In both "the one and the other vocation . . . there is operative that 'gift' that each one receives from God, that is, the grace" of God. But everyone must remain "faithful to his gift" (297). If "anyone chooses marriage, he must choose it just as it was instituted by the Creator 'in the beginning.'...If on the other hand anyone decides to pursue continence for the kingdom of heaven, he must seek in it the values proper to such a vocation" (280).

## 7. Complementarity of Marriage and Celibacy

Marriage and celibacy do not conflict. They're meant to "explain and complete each other" (276).

- Marriage reveals the nuptial character of the celibate vocation just as the celibate vocation reveals the sacramentality of marriage.
- Celibacy for the kingdom is not a sacrament because it is an anticipation of the life *beyond* sacraments.
- In the "already-but not yet" of earthly existence, celibacy stresses the "already" and marriage stresses the "not yet."

**7a.** In "the life of an authentically Christian community the attitudes and values proper to one and the other state . . . in a certain sense interpenetrate each other" (277).

**7b.** "Perfect conjugal love must be marked by that fidelity and that donation to the only Spouse . . . on which religious profession and priestly celibacy are founded." Hence, "the nature of one and the other love is 'conjugal,' that is, expressed through the total gift of oneself" (277).

**7c.** Although "continence 'for the sake of the kingdom of heaven' is identified with the renunciation of marriage, [it] serves indirectly to highlight what is most lasting and most profoundly personal in the vocation to marriage" (286). Therefore, "this renunciation is at the same time a particular form of affirmation of that value from which the unmarried person consistently abstains" (285).

**7d.** It is precisely "with regard to this [eschatological] dimension and this orientation" that "continence 'for the kingdom of heaven' has a particular importance and special eloquence for those who live a married life" (277).

**7e.** "Both [vocations] furnish a full answer to one of man's fundamental questions, the question about the significance of 'being a body,' that is, about the significance of masculinity and femininity" (299).

**7f.** "In order for man to be fully aware of what he is choosing (continence for the sake of the kingdom), he must also be fully aware of what he is renouncing" (285).

## 8. Celibacy Expresses the Nuptial Meaning of the Body

No one can escape the nuptial meaning of his body without doing violence to his humanity created male and female in God's image.

- Celibacy *is not* a rejection of the deep meaning of sexuality, but a living it out in an even fuller, more profound way.
- Every man is called in some way to be both a husband and a father.

- Every woman is called in some way to be both a wife and a mother.

**8a.** "Whoever . . . correctly 'comprehends' the call to continence for the kingdom of heaven and responds to it . . . preserves the integral truth of his own humanity without losing along the way any of the essential elements of the vocation of the person created [male and female] in 'God's image and likeness.'" Continence for the kingdom points to "the authentic development of the image and likeness of God in its trinitarian meaning, that is, precisely of 'communion'" (273).

**8b.** The nuptial meaning of the body reveals that the human person is created to be a gift "for" the other. Christ's words about celibacy "consequently show that this 'for,' present from the beginning at the basis of marriage, can also be at the basis of continence 'for' the kingdom of heaven" (284).

**8c.** "On the basis of the same disposition of the personal subject and on the basis of the same nuptial meaning of being, as a body, male or female, there can be formed the love that commits man to marriage for the whole duration of his life, but there can be formed also the love that commits man to a life of continence 'for the sake of the kingdom of heaven'" (284).

**8d.** Celibacy for the kingdom "has acquired the significance of an act of nuptial love, that is, a nuptial giving of oneself for the purpose of reciprocating in a particular way the nuptial love of the Redeemer; a giving of oneself understood as renunciation, but made above all out of love" (282).

**8e.** Celibacy for the kingdom "comes about on the basis of full consciousness of the nuptial meaning which masculinity and femininity contain in themselves. If this choice should come about by way of some artificial 'prescinding' from this real wealth of every human subject, it would not appropriately and adequately correspond to the content of Christ's words" (284).

**8f.** "Only in relation to [the nuptial] meaning of the masculinity and femininity of the human person does the call to voluntary continence 'for the sake of the kingdom of heaven' find full warranty and motivation. Only and exclusively in this perspective does Christ say, 'He who is able to receive this, let him receive it' (Mt 19:12)" (283).

**8g.** Continence for the kingdom "indicates the eschatological 'virginity' of the risen man, in whom there will be revealed . . . the absolute and eternal nuptial meaning of the glorified body in union with God Himself through the 'face to face' vision of Him" (267).

**8h.** Man and woman "become gifts to one another through their masculinity and femininity, also through their physical union. Continence means a conscious and voluntary renouncement of that union and all that is connected to it." Yet, the celibate person "has the knowledge of being able in that way to fulfill himself 'differently' and, in a certain way, 'more' than through matrimony, becoming a 'true gift to others' (GS 24)" (274).

## 9. Joseph and Mary's Marriage / Spiritual Fruitfulness

"Joseph, son of David, do not fear to take Mary as your wife, for that which is conceived in her is of the Holy Spirit" (Mt 1:20).

- The marriage of Joseph and Mary embraces the heavenly "marriage" and the earthly marriage simultaneously.
- In turn, their virginal marriage literally effected the marriage of heaven and earth.
- Their marriage brings *original man* and *eschatological* man together in *history*.
- Their superabundant spiritual fruitfulness effects the "hypostatic union."

NOTES

- All men and women who live an authentic life of celibacy "for the kingdom" participate in some way in this superabundant fruitfulness.

**9a.** "The marriage of Mary and Joseph conceals within itself, at the same time, the *mystery* of the perfect communion of the persons, of the man and woman in the conjugal pact, and also the mystery of that singular continence for the kingdom of heaven: a continence that served, in the history of salvation, the most perfect 'fruitfulness of the Holy Spirit.' Indeed, it was in a certain sense the absolute fullness of that spiritual fruitfulness since precisely in [their celibate] marriage . . . there was realized the gift of the Incarnation" (268).

**9b.** "Mary and Joseph . . . became the first witnesses of a fruitfulness different from that of the flesh, that is, of a fruitfulness of the Spirit: 'That which is conceived in her is of the Holy Spirit' (Mt 1:20)" (268).

**9c.** Celibacy "'for the kingdom of heaven' must lead in its normal development to 'paternity' or 'maternity' in a spiritual sense. . . . For its part, physical procreation also fully responds to its meaning only if it is completed by paternity and maternity in the spirit" (278).

**9d.** "Though [Christ] is born of her like every other man, . . . nonetheless Mary's maternity is virginal. To this virginal maternity of Mary there corresponds the virginal mystery of Joseph" (268).

**9e.** "*In this family, Joseph is the father: his fatherhood* is not one that derives from begetting offspring; but neither is it an 'apparent' or merely 'substitute' fatherhood. Rather, it is one that *fully shares in authentic human fatherhood*" (RC, n. 21).

# Cycle 5: The Sacramentality of Marriage

(TB, pp. 304-368)

In these 22 general audience addresses delivered between July 28, 1982 and February 9, 1983, John Paul applies his "total vision of man" to deepening our understanding of the sacrament of marriage. Reflecting on the following passage from Ephesians 5, John Paul seeks to uncover the divine dimension of "covenant and grace" and the human dimension of the "sacramental sign." This cycle is a crowning of the "triptych" of Christ's words that form the basis of the theology of the body.

> Be subject to one another out of reverence for Christ. Wives, be subject to your husbands, as to the Lord. For the husband is the head of the wife as Christ is the head of the church, his body, and is himself its Savior. As the church is subject to Christ, so let wives also be subject in everything to their husbands. Husbands, love your wives, as Christ loved the church and gave himself up for her, that he might sanctify her, having cleansed her by the washing of water with the word, that he might present the church to himself in splendor, without spot or wrinkle or any such thing, that she might be holy and without blemish. Even so husbands should love their wives as their own bodies. He who loves his wife loves himself. For no man ever hates his own flesh, but nourishes and cherishes it, as Christ does the church, because we are members of his body. "For this reason a man shall leave his father and mother and be joined to his wife, and the two shall become one flesh." This is a great mystery, and I mean in reference to Christ and the church; however, let each one of you love his wife as himself, and let the wife see that she respects her husband (Eph 5:21-33).

## 1. The Crowning of the Truths of Scripture

The above "key and classic text" takes us to the threshold of the meaning and mystery of the universe, to the threshold of discovering the glory and greatness that God has bestowed on us by creating us as male and female and calling us to become "one flesh."

- It isn't coincidental that in our day this passage is often vehemently contested.
- Here we glimpse the great clash of two competing humanisms and their respective views of the human body and the meaning of sexuality.
- Nor is it coincidental that this passage is followed by the call to take up arms in the great "spiritual battle" — Gird your loins with the truth (see Eph 6:14)!

**1a.** We should consider this passage "as the 'crowning' of the themes and truths which, through the word of God revealed in Sacred Scripture, ebb and flow like long waves" (305).

**1b.** The "great mystery" proclaimed in Ephesians 5 is understood "as God's salvific plan in regard to humanity." This "is in a certain sense the central theme of the whole of revelation, its central reality. It is this that God, as Creator and Father, wishes above all to transmit to mankind in His Word" (322).

**1c.** The text of Ephesians 5 "reveals — in a particular way — man to man, and makes him aware of his lofty vocation" (306). It "appears as the compendium or *summa*, in some sense, *of the teaching about God and man* which was brought to fulfillment by Christ" (LF, n. 19).

**1d.** We must try "to understand possibly 'to the very depths' how much richness of the truth revealed by God is contained in the scope of [this] wonderful page" (306). Here we are "witnesses of a particular meeting of [the divine] mystery with the very essence of the vocation to marriage" (311).

**1e.** "We must recognize the logic of this marvelous text which radically frees our way of thinking from elements of Manichaeism or from a non-personalistic consideration of the body" (378). What we learn here is that "carnal love" is meant to express "the language of 'agape'" (320).

## 2. The Head/Body Analogy

"For the husband is the head of the wife as Christ is the head of the church, his body. . . . Even so, husbands should loves their wives as their own bodies. He who loves his wife loves himself" (Eph 5:23, 28).

- The head-body analogy presents spouses as "one organic union" — "one organism" (see 315).
- If the body expresses the person, by becoming "one body," spouses become in some sense "one person" or "one subject" — but *without blurring their individuality.*
- Recall that Christ says any proper "headship" among His followers must not be modeled after the Gentiles who "lord it over" their subjects and make their authority felt. Instead the "lord" must be the servant (see Lk 22:25-26).

**2a.** Conjugal love is so unifying that it allows spouses "to be mutually interpenetrated, spiritually belonging to one another to such a degree that the . . . 'I' becomes in a certain sense the 'you' and the 'you' the 'I'" (320). "The 'I' of the wife . . . becomes through love the 'I' of the husband" (319).

**2b.** Spouses are "undivided in spirit and flesh, truly two in one flesh. Where the flesh is one, one also is the spirit" (CCC, n. 1642).

**2c.** "This analogy however does not blur the individuality of the subjects" (316). "There is no doubt that Christ is a subject different from the Church; however, in virtue of a particular relationship, He is united with her as an organic union of head and body" (315). Therefore, the spouses' "uni-subjectivity is based on bi-subjectivity and has not a real character but only intentional" (319).

## 3. The Spousal Analogy

"The analogy of body-head becomes the analogy of groom-bride" (314). "*As* the church, . . . so let wives; *as* Christ . . . so husbands" (Eph 5:24-28).

- According to the analogy, the wife is an icon of the Church and the husband is an icon of Christ.
- The analogy obviously breaks down (e.g., no husband is a perfect image of Christ), yet it speaks volumes about the nature of marriage and of Christ's love for us.

**3a.** In the Old Testament the "mystery which is expressed and, in a certain sense, explained by" the spousal analogy "is scarcely outlined, 'half-open' as it were; in the letter to the Ephesians, however, it is fully revealed (but of course without ceasing to be a mystery)" (329-330).

**3b.** "The analogy of spousal love contains in itself a characteristic of the mystery which is not directly emphasized . . . by any other analogy used in the Bible" (331).

**3c.** St. Paul presents "the union of Christ with the Church . . . under the simile of marriage, of the conjugal union of husband and wife." In "this case, it is not merely a comparison in a metaphorical sense" (341). The "analogy of spousal or conjugal love helps to penetrate the very essence of the mystery" (330).

**3d.** "It is obvious that the analogy of earthly . . . spousal love cannot provide an adequate and complete understanding of that absolute transcendent Reality which is the divine mystery." It helps us "to understand it up to a certain point — naturally in an analogical way. . . . The mystery remains transcendent in regard to this analogy as in regard to any other analogy, whereby we seek to express it in human language. At the same time, however, this analogy offers the possibility of a certain . . . 'penetration' into the very essence of the mystery" (330).

**3e.** In "the very essence of marriage a particle of the mystery is captured. Otherwise, the entire analogy would hang suspended in a void." (313).

**3f.** The spousal analogy "operates in two directions." It "helps us better to understand the essence of the relationship between Christ and the Church [and], at the same time, it helps us to see more deeply into the essence of marriage." In fact, "at the basis of an understanding of marriage in its very essence is the spousal relationship of Christ to the Church." In turn, marriage "becomes a visible sign of the divine eternal mystery, as an image of the Church united with Christ. In this way the letter to the Ephesians leads us to the very foundations of the sacramentality of marriage" (313).

**3g.** We "see how profoundly the author of the letter to the Ephesians examines the sacramental reality, proclaiming its grand analogy: both the union of Christ with the Church, and the conjugal union of man and woman in marriage are in this way illuminated by a particular supernatural light" (318).

## 4. Mutual Subjection

"Be subject to one another out of reverence for Christ. As the church is subject to Christ, so let wives also be subject in everything to their husbands. Husbands, love your wives, as Christ loved the church and gave himself up for her" (Eph 5:21, 24-25).

- Void of "the gift" the feminist revolt against Ephesians 5 is quite understandable. They see it as a surrender to tyranny. But we are not void of the gift!
- The gift is that Christ came not to *be* served *but to serve* — and to lay down His life for His Bride (see Mt 20:28). God is not a tyrant!
- St. Paul *does not justify male domination*. This is the result of sin (see Gn 3:16).
- He is actually calling husbands and wives to live "the gift" of God's original plan in which there was a perfect balance, complementarity, and equality between the sexes.
- In effect, Paul says subjection means one thing to the Gentiles, but it must be *very* different for Christians.
- The mutual relationship of spouses must flow from their common relationship with Christ (see 309).

**4a.** St. Paul "does not fear to accept those concepts which were characteristic of the mentality and of the customs of the times. . . . Nowadays our contemporary sensitivity is certainly different; quite different, too [is] the social position of women in regard to men" (310-311).

**4b.** Christians "must no longer live as the Gentiles do." They "are darkened in their understanding . . . due to their hardness of heart." So put off "your old nature which . . . is corrupt through deceitful lusts, . . . and be renewed in the spirit of your minds, and put on the new nature, created after the likeness of God in true righteousness and holiness" (Eph 4:17-18, 22-24).

**4c.** To be "subject" to one's spouse means to be "completely given" (312). In turn, mutual subjection means "a reciprocal donation of self." When "Christ is the source and at the same time the model of that subjection [it] confers on the conjugal union a profound and mature character" (310).

**4d.** When Paul says "be subject to your husbands as to the Lord" (Eph 5:22), he "does not intend to say that the husband is 'lord' of the wife [in any way that would imply] that the interpersonal pact proper to marriage is a pact of domination of the husband over the wife" (310).

**4e.** The love to which St. Paul calls husbands clearly "excludes every kind of subjection whereby the wife might become a servant or a slave of the husband, an object of unilateral domination. Love makes the husband simultaneously subject to the wife, and thereby to the Lord Himself, just as the wife to the husband" (310).

**4f.** In imaging Christ and the Church, "the husband is above all *he who loves*, and the wife, on the other hand is *she who is loved*." Thus, we can conclude that "the wife's 'submission' to her husband, understood in the context of the entire passage. . . , signifies above all 'the experiencing of love.' All the more so since this 'submission' is related to the image of the submission of the Church to Christ, which certainly consists in experiencing His love" (320).

**4g.** "So therefore that 'reverence for Christ' and 'respect' of which [St. Paul] speaks, is none other than a spiritually mature form of that mutual attraction: man's attraction to femininity and woman's attraction to masculinity" (379).

**4h.** If a husband is truly to love his wife, "it is necessary to insist that intercourse must not serve merely as a means of allowing [his] climax. . . . The man must take [the] difference between male and female reactions into account . . . so that climax may be reached [by] both . . . and as far as possible occur in both simultaneously." The husband must do this "not for hedonistic, but for altruistic reasons" (LR, p. 272). In this case, if "we take into account the shorter and more violent curve of arousal in the man, [such] tenderness on his part in the context of marital intercourse acquires the significance of an act of virtue" (LR, p. 275).

## 5. Physical Beauty as a Metaphor for Holiness

Christ "gave himself up for her . . . that she might be holy and without blemish" (Eph 5:25-27).

- A beautiful body, for St. Paul, expresses spiritual beauty — holiness.
- Christ loved His Bride when she was full of the "blemishes" of sin.
- He took on her "ugliness" so that she might be "beautiful."
- What is the element of truth in our culture's quest for the "ideal" body?

**5a.** "It is significant that the image of the Church 'in splendor' is presented . . . as a bride all beautiful in her body. Certainly this is a metaphor; but it is very eloquent and it shows how deeply important is the body in the analogy of spousal love" (318).

**5b.** For St. Paul, the human body indicates "attributes and qualities of the moral, spiritual, and supernatural order." He is able to penetrate the mystery of redemption "by means of the resemblance of the body and of the love whereby husband and wife become 'one flesh'" (318-319).

**5c.** It is Christ who will "present the Church to himself" (Eph 5:27) in radiance. This "seems to indicate that moment of the wedding in which the bride is led to the groom, already clothed in the bridal dress and adorned for the wedding. The text quoted indicates that the Christ-spouse Himself takes care to adorn the spouse-Church; He is concerned that she should be beautiful with the beauty of grace, beautiful by virtue of the gift of salvation in its fullness, already granted from the moment of the sacrament of baptism" (317).

**5d.** "Love obliges the bridegroom-husband to be solicitous for the welfare of the bride-wife, it commits him to desire her beauty and at the same time to appreciate this beauty and to care for it. Here it is a case of visible beauty, of physical beauty" (319).

**5e.** "Giving himself in the most disinterested way" the "bridegroom examines his bride with attention, as though in a creative loving anxiety to find everything that is good and beautiful in her." This is what "he desires for her." Through his love he "creates" the goodness that he sees in the one he loves. The husband's ability to see that good "is like a test of that same love and its measure" (319).

## 6. Sacrament, Mystery, and Sign

The "great mystery" of God is made visible through the economy of sacramental signs.

- "Sacrament" — in the more ancient, broader meaning of the word — refers to the revelation and accomplishment of the eternal mystery hidden in God (see 341).
- "Mystery" is the only word we can utter to speak of the invisible, divine reality.
- Together, these words — "mystery-sacrament" — refer to the "hidden-revealed" dimensions of God and His plan for humanity.
- "Sign" simply means the "visibility of the Invisible" (see 332). However, we must always be careful not to reduce the divine reality to its sign.
- The *good news* of the Gospel is that that which was "hidden" in God from eternity has been revealed — first through the sign of man and woman's original unity and *definitively* through the sign of the union of Christ and the Church.

**6a.** "Is not 'sacrament' synonymous with 'mystery'? The mystery remains . . . hidden in God Himself — in such [a way] that even after its proclamation (or its revelation) it does not cease to be called 'mystery'" (323).

**6b.** Participation in the eternal plan of God "becomes a reality in a mysterious way, under the veil of a sign; nonetheless, that sign is always a 'making visible' of the supernatural mystery which it works in man under its veil" (323).

**6c.** Even "if in the most general way, the body enters the definition of sacrament, being 'a visible sign of the invisible reality,' that is, of the spiritual, transcendent, divine reality. In this sign — and through this sign — God gives Himself to man in His transcendent truth and in His love. The sacrament is a sign [which] effectively contributes to having grace become part of man, and to realizing and fulfilling in him the work of salvation, the work begun by God from all eternity and fully revealed in Jesus Christ" (305-306).

**6d.** "The sacrament consists in the 'manifesting' of that mystery in a sign which serves not only to proclaim the mystery, but also to accomplish it in man. The sacrament is a visible and efficacious sign of grace. Through it, there is accomplished in man that mystery hidden from eternity in God, of which the letter to the Ephesians speaks" (323).

**6e.** "The body in fact, and only it, is capable of making visible what is invisible: the spiritual and divine. It was created to transfer into the visible reality of the world the mystery hidden from eternity in God, and thus to be its sign" (335).

**6f.** Through "the image of the conjugal union of husband and wife, the author of [Ephesians] speaks . . . of the way in which that mystery is expressed in the visible order, of the way in which it has become visible, and therefore has entered into the sphere of sign" (332).

## 7. Man was "Chosen in Christ" from the Beginning

The Father "has blessed us in Christ with every spiritual blessing . . . even as he chose us in him before the foundation of the world" (Eph 1:3-4).

- This means that God the Father chose us in Christ not *only* after we sinned and not *only* in order to redeem us from sin.
- The Incarnate Christ "is the center of the universe and of history" (RH, n. 1).
- It seems in John Paul's perspective that the Incarnation should not be considered an afterthought — a second plan intended to rectify the first which was supposedly thwarted when man sinned.
- God's *eternal* plan is to unite us with Christ and sin cannot thwart it. God's plan for man and for the universe continues despite sin.

**7a.** "At the heart of the mystery there is Christ. In Him — precisely in Him — humanity has been eternally blessed 'with every spiritual blessing.' In Him — in Christ — humanity has been chosen 'before the creation of the world.'" When "this eternal mystery is accomplished in time, this is brought about also in Him and through Him: in Christ and through Christ. Through Christ there is revealed the mystery of divine love. Through Him and in Him it is accomplished." Furthermore, "Christ Himself is the gift: He gives Himself to the Church as to His spouse" (325).

**7b.** "The letter to the Ephesians opens up before us the supernatural world . . . of the eternal plans of God the Father concerning man. These plans precede . . . the creation of man." Original holiness demonstrates that "before sin, man bore in his soul the fruit of eternal election in Christ. . . . Man, male and female, shared from the 'beginning' in this supernatural gift. This bounty was granted in consideration of Him . . . even though — according to the dimensions of time and history — it had preceded the Incarnation" (334).

**7c.** "The redemption was to become the source of man's supernatural endowment after sin and, in a certain sense, in spite of sin. This supernatural endowment, which took place before original sin . . . was accomplished precisely in reference to Him . . . while anticipating chronologically His coming in the body" (335).

**7d.** The "mystery of Christ casts conclusive light on the mystery of creation and reveals the end for which 'in the beginning God created the heavens and the earth': from the beginning, God envisaged the glory of the new creation in Christ" (CCC, n. 280).

**7e.** Marriage "should serve not only to prolong the work of creation [through] procreation, but also to extend to further generations . . . the supernatural fruits of man's eternal election . . . in the eternal Son" (336).

**7f.** "Marriage . . . is an efficacious expression of the saving power of God who accomplishes His eternal plan even after sin and in spite of . . . concupiscence" (347).

## 8. The "Sacrament of Creation" Is Linked to the "Sacrament of Redemption"

"'For this reason a man shall leave his father and mother and be joined to his wife, and the two shall become one flesh.' This is a great mystery, and I mean in reference to Christ and the Church" (Eph 5:31-32).

- There is a sign which "sums up" the mystery of creation and a sign which "sums up" the mystery of redemption — the union of the first Adam and Eve, and of the second.
- The union of husband and wife in the totality of the "sacrament of creation" is the most ancient sign of the mystery.
- And the union of Christ and the Church in the totality of the "sacrament of redemption" is the definitive sign of this mystery revealed in "the fullness of time."

**8a.** The linking of the "one flesh" union of marriage with the union of Christ and the Church "is the most important point of the whole text, in a certain sense, the keystone" (321). "It is of special merit [that St. Paul] brought these two signs together, and made of them one great sign — that is, a great sacrament" (333).

**8b.** In this linking, St. Paul "unites marriage, as the most ancient revelation ('manifestation') of the [divine] plan in the created world, with the definitive revelation and 'manifestation'" of that plan in Jesus Christ. In this way "St. Paul sets in relief the continuity between the most ancient covenant . . . and the definitive covenant. . . . This continuity . . . constitutes the essential basis of the great analogy contained in the letter to the Ephesians" (321-322).

**8c.** "So the mystery hidden in God from all eternity . . . in the sacrament of creation, became *a visible reality through the union* of the first man and woman in the perspective of marriage." This same mystery "becomes in the sacrament of redemption *a visible reality [through] the indissoluble union of Christ with the Church*, which the author of the letter to the Ephesians presents as the nuptial union of spouses" (338).

**8d.** "As the 'first Adam' — man, male and female — created in the state of original innocence and called in this state to conjugal union (in this sense we are speaking of the sacrament of creation) was a sign of the eternal mystery, so the 'second Adam,' Christ, united with the Church through the sacrament of redemption by an indissoluble bond, analogous to the indissoluble bond of spouses, is a definitive sign of the same eternal mystery" (338).

**8e.** "It can be said that the visible sign of marriage 'in the beginning,' inasmuch as it linked to the visible sign of Christ and of the Church, to the summit of the salvific economy of God, transfers the eternal plan of love into the 'historical' dimension and makes it the foundation of the whole sacramental order" (332-333).

**8f.** In "*speaking about the eternal mystery being actuated*, we are speaking *also about the fact that it becomes visible with the visibility of the sign*." And therefore, with regard to these signs, "we are speaking . . . in reference to the entire work of creation and redemption" (338-339).

## 9. The Original Gracing and the New Gracing

The *original gracing* refers to man and woman's participation in divine life according to the "sacrament of creation" and the *new gracing* according to the "sacrament of redemption."

- In the beginning grace was poured out on man through the "primordial sacrament."

- Marriage was the "unique sacrament" for the man of innocence (see 340), but marriage lost its ability to confer grace as a result of original sin.
- Even so, conjugal union continued to mold history as a "figure" of the original sacrament and remained the "platform for the actuation of God's designs" (336).
- The longing for "beatifying union" which we all experience as reminiscent of the "original gracing" prepares men and women for the "new gracing" of redemption.
- Grace is now poured out on man through the spousal union of Christ and the Church made present in the seven sacraments.

**9a.** The "marriage of the first husband and wife [was] a sign of the [original] gracing of man in the sacrament of creation." This "corresponds [to] the marriage, or rather the analogy of the marriage, of Christ with the Church [which serves] as the fundamental 'great' sign of the [new] gracing of man in the sacrament of redemption" (337).

**9b.** There is an essential "continuity" and "difference" between the original and the new gracing. The "original gracing . . . constituted that man . . . in the state of original innocence and justice. The new gracing of man . . . gives him above all 'the remission of sins.' Yet even here grace can 'abound even more'" (337).

**9c.** The Apostle's linking of the original union of spouses with the union of Christ and the Church speaks "of a real *renewal* (or of a 're-creation,' that is, of a new creation) of *that which constituted the salvific content* . . . of the primordial sacrament" (341).

**9d.** "Marriage as a primordial sacrament constitutes . . . the *figure* (and so: the likeness, the analogy) according to which there is constructed the basic . . . structure of the new economy of salvation" (339).

**9e.** "In this new sacrament of redemption, marriage is organically inscribed, just as it was inscribed in the original sacrament of creation" (353). Indeed, through "the new covenant of Christ with the Church, marriage is again inscribed in that 'sacrament of man' which embraces the universe" (354).

**9f.** Marriage arises "from redemption *in the form . . . of a 'prototype'*. . . . Reflecting deeply on this dimension, one would have to conclude that all the sacraments of the new covenant find in a certain sense their prototype in marriage as the primordial sacrament" (339).

**9g.** "The entire Christian life bears the mark of the spousal love of Christ and the Church. Already Baptism . . . is a nuptial mystery; it is so to speak the nuptial bath which precedes the wedding feast, the Eucharist" (CCC, n. 1617). "*The Eucharist is the . . . sacrament of the Bridegroom and the Bride*" (MD, n. 26).

## 10. The Spousal Significance of the Body Is Completed by the Redemptive Significance

The nuptial meaning of the body expressed in the union of the first Adam and Eve takes on a redemptive significance in the union of the New Adam and Eve.

- The nuptial meaning of the body reveals that we are called to love as God loves.
- However, we cannot fulfill this without experiencing the redemption of the body.
- The redemption of the body is accomplished as Christ fulfills the body's nuptial meaning in becoming a "sincere gift" to His Bride.

**10a.** "The Pauline image of marriage . . . brings together the redemptive dimension and the spousal dimension of love. In a certain sense it fuses these two dimensions into one. Christ . . . has married the Church as a bride, because 'he has given himself up for her' (Eph 5:25). Through the sacrament of marriage, both these dimensions of love, the spousal and the redemptive, . . . permeate the life of the spouses" (352).

**10b.** Marriage "corresponds to the vocation of Christians only when it reflects the love which Christ the Bridegroom gives to the Church His Bride, and which the Church . . . attempts to return to Christ. This is redeeming love, love as salvation, the love with which man from eternity has been loved by God in Christ" (312).

**10c.** The "'great mystery' of the union of Christ to the Church obliges us to link the spousal significance of the body with its redemptive significance." This link is obviously "important with regard to marriage and to the Christian vocation of husbands and wives." However it "is equally essential and valid for understanding man in general: for the fundamental problem of understanding him and for the self-comprehension of his being in the world." Indeed, it is in this link that we "find the answer to the question concerning the meaning of 'being a body'" (352-353).

**10d.** "Man, who 'from the beginning' is male and female, should seek the meaning of his existence and the meaning of his humanity by reaching out to the mystery of creation through the reality of redemption. . . . The union of Christ with the Church permits us to understand in what way the spousal significance of the body is completed with the redemptive significance, and . . . not only in marriage." This happens "in all the diverse ways of life and in diverse situations: . . . indeed, in the very birth and death of man" (354).

## 11. The Sacramental Sign of Marriage

Every sacrament has a specific sign that communicates the invisible reality it symbolizes.

- The sacramental sign of marriage is one of "multiple content" (363).
- It begins with the exchange of consent, is consummated in conjugal intercourse, and is borne in the spouses themselves throughout the duration of their marriage.
- Conjugal intercourse is where the words of the wedding vows become flesh.
- If all of married life is a sacramental sign, we might say that conjugal intercourse is "the sign of that sign."
- Just as the body is the sign of the soul, the "one body" spouses become is the sign in some sense of the "soul" of their married life.

**11a.** "Both of them, as man and woman, being the ministers of the sacrament in the moment of contracting marriage constitute at the same time the full and real visible sign of the sacrament itself" (356). "The man and woman as spouses, bear this sign throughout the whole of their lives and remain as that sign until death" (357).

**11b.** "All married life is a gift; but this becomes most evident when the spouses, in giving themselves to each other in love, bring about that encounter which makes them 'one flesh'" (LF, n. 12).

**11c.** "The words spoken by them would not *per se* constitute the sacramental sign of marriage unless there corresponded to them . . . the awareness of the body, linked to the masculinity and femininity of the husband and wife" (356).

NOTES

**11d.** The exchange of vows is "merely the sign of the coming into being of marriage." Without "consummation the marriage is not yet constituted in its full reality . . . as a marriage. Indeed the very words 'I take you as my wife — my husband' . . . can be fulfilled only by means of conjugal intercourse." With conjugal intercourse "we pass to the reality which corresponds to these words. Both the one and the other element are important in regard to the structure of the sacramental sign" (355).

**11e.** The "consent that binds the spouses to each other finds its fulfillment in the two 'becoming one flesh'" (CCC, n. 1627).

**11f.** The marriage covenant "constitutes the foundation of that union when '. . . they become one flesh' (Gn 2:24)." In this context "one can say that such bodily union . . . is the regular sign of the communion of . . . husband and wife" (141).

**11g.** Husband and wife are "the minister[s] of the sacrament which 'from the beginning' was constituted by the sign of the 'union of flesh'" (397).

**11h.** "The body . . . is called 'from the beginning' to become the manifestation of the spirit. It does so also by means of the conjugal union of man and woman [in] 'one flesh.'" By means of this unity, "the body, in its masculinity and femininity, assumes the value of a sign — in a way, a sacramental sign" (163).

**11i.** "The structure of the sacramental sign . . . remains essentially the same as 'in the beginning.' It is determined, in a certain sense, by 'the language of the body' inasmuch as the man and the woman, who through marriage should become one flesh, express in this sign the reciprocal gift of masculinity and femininity as the basis of the conjugal union of the persons" (356).

## 12. The Language of the Body

All that John Paul has said about the body and its nuptial meaning and marriage as a "great mystery" imaging Christ's love for the Church is expressed through the "language of the body."

- The body "speaks" the deepest truth of man's existence as male and female.
- It speaks of his call to love as God loves in a life-giving communion of persons.
- It speaks of God's love for humanity, Christ's love for the Church.

**12a.** Man "cannot, in a certain sense, express this singular language of his personal existence and of his vocation without the body." The "most profound words of the spirit — words of love, of giving, of fidelity — demand an adequate 'language of the body.' And without that, they can not be fully expressed" (359).

**12b.** In the course of married life "the spouses' bodies will speak 'for' and 'on behalf of' each of them . . . carrying out the conjugal dialogue proper to their vocation. . . . The spouses are called to form their life . . . as a 'communion of persons' on the basis of that . . . 'language of the body'" (364).

**12c.** "As ministers of a sacrament which is constituted by consent and perfected by conjugal union, man and woman are called to express that mysterious 'language' of their bodies in all the truth which is proper to it. By means of gestures and reactions, by means of the whole dynamism . . . of tension and enjoyment — whose direct source is the body in its masculinity and its femininity, the body in its action and interaction — by means of all this, . . . the person, 'speaks.' . . . Precisely on the level of this 'language of the body' . . . man and woman reciprocally express themselves in the fullest and most profound way possible to them" (397-398).

## 13. The Prophetism of the Body

A prophet is one who expresses in human words the mystery of God. The language of the body is meant to "proclaim" the "great mystery" of Christ and the Church.

- It is in this way that the language of the body is understood as "prophetic."
- We must be careful however to distinguish between true and false prophets (see 365).
- God has given us the freedom to "author" the language of our own bodies, but not to determine that language.
- If we can speak the "truth" with the body, we can also speak "lies."
- Joy and profound inner harmony come to married life only when the ongoing "dialogue" of the language of the body is honest — when spouses are "true prophets."

**13a.** When the "spouses proclaim precisely this 'language of the body,' reread in truth, [they] perform an act of prophetic character. They confirm in this way their participation in the prophetic mission of the Church received from Christ" (361). Spouses "must not forget that the 'language of the body,' before being spoken by [them] was spoken by the word of the living God" (362).

**13b.** In the spousal analogy of the prophets "it is the body itself which 'speaks'; it speaks by means of its masculinity and femininity, . . . it speaks . . . both in the language of fidelity, that is, of love, and also in the language of conjugal infidelity, that is, of 'adultery'" (359).

**13c.** "One can speak of moral good and evil" in the sexual relationship "according to whether . . . or not it has the character of the truthful sign" (141-142).

**13d.** For "every language . . . the categories of truth and non-truth . . . are essential." The body speaks the truth "through conjugal love, fidelity, and integrity." It speaks lies "by all that is the negation of conjugal love, fidelity, and integrity" (360-361).

**13e.** "We can say that the essential element for marriage as a sacrament is the 'language of the body' in its aspect of truth. It is precisely by means of that, that the sacramental sign is, in fact, constituted" (360). "A correct rereading 'in truth' is an indispensable condition to proclaim this truth, that is, to institute the visible sign of marriage as a sacrament" (361).

**13f.** Spouses "are called explicitly to bear witness — by using correctly the 'language of the body' — to spousal and procreative love, a witness worthy of 'true prophets.' In this consists the true significance and the grandeur of conjugal consent in the sacrament of the Church" (365).

**13g.** "If concupiscence . . . causes many 'errors' in rereading the language of the body and . . . gives rise also to sin . . . contrary to the virtue of chastity, . . . nevertheless in the sphere of the ethos of redemption there always remains the possibility of passing from 'error' to the 'truth'. . . the possibility of . . . conversion from sin to chastity as an expression of a life according to the [Holy] Spirit" (366-367).

# Cycle 6: Love and Fruitfulness

(TB, pp. 368-423)

The Pope postponed his catechesis on the body during the special Holy Year of Redemption in 1983. He resumed in spring of the following year with his sixth and final cycle consisting of 21 addresses delivered between May 23 and November 28, 1984. Premising some reflections on the Song of Songs, the book of Tobit, and some new themes gleaned from Ephesians 5, John Paul II applies his "adequate anthropology" to the teaching of Pope Paul VI's landmark encyclical *Humanae Vitae*.

[**Note**: Some divisions of the Pope's catechesis place the first five addresses of Cycle 6 (Love and Fruitfulness) at the conclusion of Cycle 5 (Sacramentality of Marriage). However, not only does John Paul himself indicate that these audiences are a preface of sorts to his analysis of *Humanae Vitae* (see 368), the importance of these audiences is also "felt" more when seen in this light.]

> Questions "come from [*Humanae Vitae*] that in a certain sense permeate the sum total of our reflections. It follows, then, that this last [cycle] is not artificially added to the sum total, but is organically and homogeneously united with it" (422). In fact, the entire catechesis on the body can be considered "an ample commentary on the doctrine contained in the encyclical *Humanae Vitae*" (420).

## 1. The Biblical Ode to Erotic Love

"All scripture [including the Song of Songs] is inspired by God and profitable for teaching, for reproof, for correction, and for training in righteousness" (2 Tm: 3:16).

- Quoting from various scholars, John Paul seems critical of those who rush to disembody the Song of Songs, seeing it only as an allegory of God's "spiritual" love.
- He quotes one scholar who says that to "forget the lovers" or to "petrify them in fictions" is not the right way to interpret the Song of Songs (see 384).
- John Paul examines the Song to gain a "more exhaustive" understanding of the sacramental sign of marriage (see 370).
- The Song of Song witnesses to the purification of *eros* by *agape*.
- It is a love that is simultaneously spiritual and sensual (see 373) — they see, hear, feel, smell, and even taste each other (see Song 1:12-14; 2:3-6; 4:10-5:1).
- We see signs of the purity of original man, the struggle of historical man, and the longing for eschatological man.

**1a.** Because the content of the Song of Songs is "apparently 'profane' . . . its reading has often been discouraged." Yet, at the same time "it has been the source from which the greatest mystical writers have drawn and [its] verses . . . have been inserted into the Church's liturgy" (368).

**1b.** "What was expressed in the second Chapter of Genesis (vv. 23-25) in just a few simple and essential words, is developed here in a full dialogue, as it were, or rather a duet. . . . Man's first words in Genesis . . . express wonder and admiration, even more, the sense of fascination. And a similar fascination . . . runs in fuller form through the verses of the Song of Songs" (369).

**1c.** Just like in the beginning, the "point of departure as well as the point of arrival for this fascination . . . are in fact the bride's femininity and the groom's masculinity in the direct experience of their visibility. The words of love uttered by both of them are therefore concentrated on the 'body.'" It "is on the body that there lingers directly and immediately that attraction toward the other person . . . which in the interior impulse of the heart generates love" (369).

**1d.** "In addition, love unleashes a special experience of the beautiful, which focuses on what is visible, but at the same time involves the entire person. The experience of beauty gives rise to [mutual] satisfaction" (369).

## 2. My Sister, My Bride

"You have ravished my heart, my sister, my bride, you have ravished my heart with one glance of your eyes. . . . How sweet is your love, my sister, my bride!" (Song 4:9-10).

- Calling her "sister" *before* calling her "bride" has a "special eloquence" (371).
- It shows that the man's desire for the woman is not one of lust but of love.
- He sees her not as a thing to be appropriated, but as a person who shares the same humanity.
- When the term "sister" gives way to the term "bride," it does so without losing what is essential in the groom's recognition of her as "sister."

**2a.** "The expression 'sister' speaks of the union in mankind and at the same time of her difference and feminine originality" (371).

**2b.** Seeing his beloved as "sister" presents "a kind of challenge" for the man. "The groom in the Song accepts the challenge and seeks the common past." It is as if they "were descended from the same family circle, as though from infancy they were united by memories of a common home. And so they mutually feel as close as brother and sister. . . . From this there follows a specific sense of common belonging" (371).

**2c.** "The groom's words, through the name 'sister' tend to reproduce . . . the history of the femininity of the person loved. They see her still in the time of girlhood and they embrace her entire 'I,' soul and body, with a disinterested tenderness" (371).

## 3. The Woman as a "Garden Enclosed"

"A garden locked is my sister, my bride, a garden enclosed, a fountain sealed" (Song 4:12).

- This expression also demonstrates that the Lover sees the woman as a person created for "her own sake." He cannot "grasp" at her (recall the "freedom of the gift").

- If the Lover is to enter this garden, he cannot barge in or break down the door. Nor can he manipulate her into surrendering the key.
- He must entrust himself to her freedom; she might refuse. This is the man's risk.
- He puts "his hand to the latch" (Sg 5:4) only with her freely given "yes." In total freedom (without any hint of coercion) she says: "I belong to my lover."
- If a person's "love" violates the one loved, then *it is not love* and should not be called love. It is love's counterfeit — lust.

**3a.** "The metaphors . . . 'garden enclosed, fountain sealed' reveal [that the woman is] master of her own mystery" (372).

**3b.** "The 'language of the body' reread in truth keeps pace with the discovery of the interior inviolability of the person." Authentic love means "the initiation into the mystery of the person, without [ever] implying its violation" (372, 373).

**3c.** "When the bride says, 'My lover belongs to me,' she means at the same time, 'It is he to whom I entrust myself,' and therefore she says, 'and I to him' (Sg 2:16). The words 'to me' and 'to him' affirm here the whole depth of that entrustment, which corresponds to the interior truth of the person" (372).

## 4. Tobiah and Sarah and the Test of Life and Death

"You made Adam and gave him Eve his wife. . . . And now, O Lord, I am not taking this sister of mine because of lust, but with sincerity. Grant that I may find mercy and grow old together with her. And [Sarah] said with him, 'Amen'" (Tb 8: 6-8).

- Tobiah sets his heart on God's original plan for marriage. He calls her "sister." He contrasts lust with the sincere gift of self. He knows that he needs God's mercy to live the truth and he longs to spend his whole life with her.
- In receiving this mercy, they consummate their marriage and Tobiah lives!
- If the demon in Sarah's previous marriages wrote death into the plan of man and woman's relationship, the angel's message to Tobiah restored life to that plan.
- In the face of authentic nuptial love, death has no chance. Life refuses to surrender!
- Their union joyously proclaims: "Where O death, is your victory? Where, O death, is your sting?" (1 Co 15:55).

**4a.** Spouses, "becoming one as husband and wife, find themselves in the situation in which the powers of good and evil fight and compete against each other." The "choices and the actions [of men and women] take on all the weight of human existence in the union of the two" (376).

**4b.** Tobiah and Sarah "unhesitatingly face this test. But in this test of life and death, life wins because, during the test on the wedding night, love, supported by prayer, is revealed as more stern than death." Love "is victorious because it prays" (376).

**4c.** "The truth and the power of love are shown in the ability to place oneself between the forces of good and evil which are fighting in man and around him, because love is confident in the victory of good and is ready to do everything so that good may conquer" (376).

## 5. The Language of the Body Becomes Liturgical

With all that we've said about marriage as a sacramental participation in the "great mystery" of Jesus Christ, it shouldn't surprise us that John Paul speaks of conjugal life as being "liturgical."

- The Church celebrates her liturgy especially in and through the sacraments.
- Recall that marriage is in some sense the "prototype" of all of the sacraments.
- Not only is conjugal life "liturgical," but the Church's liturgical life is in some sense "conjugal" (see CCC, n. 1617).
- Conjugal union is meant to be a great prayer of thanksgiving — it is in this sense "eucharistic."
- The marital bed can be viewed as an altar upon which spouses offer their bodies in living sacrifice, holy and acceptable to God. This is their spiritual act of worship (see Ro 12:1; see also CCC, n. 2031).

**5a.** Liturgy "means the participation of the People of God in 'the work of God'" (CCC, n. 1069). It is the Church's "celebration of divine worship." The liturgy "involves the presentation of man's sanctification under the guise of signs perceptible by the senses and its accomplishment in ways appropriate to each of these signs" (CCC, n. 1070).

**5b.** The "'language of the body reread in the subjective [and] 'objective' dimension[s] . . . becomes the language of the liturgy" (377).

**5c.** "This seems to be the integral significance of the sacramental sign of marriage. In that sign — through the 'language of the body' — man and woman encounter the 'great mystery.' . . . In this way conjugal life becomes in a certain sense liturgical" (380).

**5d.** It is the liturgy which "elevates the conjugal pact of man and woman, based on the 'language of the body' reread in truth, to the dimensions of 'mystery,' and at the same time enables that pact to be fulfilled in these dimensions through the 'language of the body.' It is precisely the sign of the sacrament of marriage that speaks of this." (378).

## 6. The Inseparable Meanings of the Conjugal Act

The teaching of *Humanae Vitae* "is founded upon the inseparable connection, established by God which man on his own initiative may not break, between the unitive significance and the procreative significance which are both inherent to the marriage act" (HV, n. 12).

- John Paul's reflections center on this passage.
- To focus on the "significance" (or meaning) of the act rather than its "end" is to evaluate the sexual act from the interior perspective of the persons performing it.
- This doesn't mean spouses are free to assign their own meaning to the act.

- Its meaning is already written by God into the "fundamental structure" of the act and the "actual nature" of man and woman (see HV, n. 12).

**6a.** "One can detect in this part of the encyclical *a very significant passage from what some might call a 'theology of nature' to a 'theology of person'*" (PC, p. 308).

**6b.** "In this renewed formulation the traditional teaching on the purposes of marriage (and their hierarchy) is reaffirmed and at the same time deepened from the viewpoint of the interior life of the spouses, that is, of conjugal and family spirituality" (407).

**6c.** The "conjugal act 'signifies' not only love, but also potential fecundity, and therefore . . . it is not licit to separate the unitive aspect from the procreative aspect, because both the one and the other pertain to the intimate truth of the conjugal act: the one is activated together with the other and in a certain sense . . . by means of the other" (398).

**6d.** When the unitve and procreative meanings are willfully separated "there is [still] carried out . . . a real bodily union, but it does not correspond to the interior truth and to the dignity of [the] communion of persons. . . . Such a violation of the interior order of conjugal union, which is rooted in the very order of the person, constitutes the essential evil of the contraceptive act" (398).

## 7. Authentic Pastoral Concern

It is often said that the Church's teaching against contraception isn't "pastoral."

- Paul VI is solicitous of the real problems and questions of modern man throughout and states explicitly that he has no desire to pass over them in silence (see HV, n. 3).
- He acknowledges that some might find the encyclical's teaching "gravely difficult" if not "impossible to observe" (see HV, n. 20).
- He states plainly, in fact, that men and women cannot live this teaching without the help of God's grace (see HV, n. 20).
- Paul VI's choice was either to trust in God's grace, or to compromise the truth.
- What is the truly loving, the truly "pastoral" thing to do?

**7a.** "Whoever believes that the . . . encyclical [does] not sufficiently take into account the difficulties present in concrete life does not understand the pastoral concern that was at [its] origin" (392).

**7b.** "Pastoral concern means the search for the true good of man, a promotion of the values engraved in his person by God; that is, it means observing the 'rule of understanding' which is directed to the ever clearer discovery of God's plan for human love, in the certitude that the only true good of the human person consists in fulfilling this divine plan" (392).

**7c.** "To diminish in no way the saving teaching of Christ constitutes an eminent form of charity for souls" (HV, n. 29).

## 8. Falsification of the Sign

We can argue against contraception entirely from philosophy and natural law, but John Paul's catechesis shows the deepest *theological* reason for the immorality of contraception — it is a falsification of the sacramental sign of married love.

- Insert contraception into the language of the body and (knowingly or unknowingly) a couple engages in a *counter-sign* of the "great mystery" — an anti-sacrament.
- In this way spouses (knowingly or unknowingly) become "false prophets." They blaspheme. They speak not the *symbolic* Word, but the *diabolic* anti-Word.

**8a.** The teaching of *Humanae Vitae* "is closely connected with our previous reflections on *marriage in its dimension as a (sacramental) sign*" (386).

**8b.** "One can speak of moral good and evil" in the sexual relationship "according to whether . . . or not it has the character of the truthful sign" (141-142).

**8c.** It "has already been said several times that [the sacramental sign] is based on the *'language of the body' reread in truth.*" During conjugal intercourse, "*a moment so rich in significance*, it is also especially important that the 'language of the body' be reread in truth" (387).

**8d.** The language of the body has "clear-cut meanings" all of which are "'programmed' . . . in the conjugal consent." For example, to "the question: 'Are you willing to accept responsibly and with love the children that God may give you . . . ?' — the man and the woman reply: 'Yes'" (363, 364).

**8e.** Authentic conjugal love "allows the building of the whole life of the married couple according to that 'truth of the sign,' by means of which marriage is built up in its sacramental dignity" (406).

**8f.** Those who live the "ethos of redemption" experience "a salvific fear . . . of violating or degrading what bears in itself the sign of the divine mystery of creation and redemption" (416).

## 9. Responsible Parenthood

Does the Church teach that couples are to leave the number of children they have entirely to "chance"? No.

- Both the teaching of Vatican II and *Humanae Vitae*, in calling couples to a responsible love, call them also to a responsible parenthood.
- In order for parenthood to be "responsible," the decision to avoid sexual union during the fertile time *or* to engage in it must not be motivated by *selfishness*.
- Natural family planning must always be understood based on the "integral intention" presented by *Humanae Vitae*.

**9a.** In the commitment to responsible parenthood one "cannot therefore speak of 'acting arbitrarily.' On the contrary the married couple 'must act in conformity with God's creative intention' (HV 10)" (394).

**9b.** Those "are considered 'to exercise responsible parenthood who prudently and generously decide to have a large family, or who, for serious reasons and with due respect to the moral law, choose to have no more children for the time being or even for an indeterminate period' (HV, n. 10)" (394).

**9c.** Responsible parenthood "involves 'common reflection and effort; it also involves [the parents'] consideration of their own good and the good of their children already born or yet to come, an ability to read the signs of the times and of their own situation on the spiritual and material level, and finally an estimation of the good of the family, of society, and of the Church' (GS, n. 50)" (393).

**9d.** The Church wisely teaches that it "is the married couple themselves who must in the last analysis arrive at these judgements before God" (GS, n. 50). This point is "of particular importance to determine . . . the moral character of 'responsible parenthood'" (393).

**9e.** Responsible parenthood "demands above all from husband and wife a definite family and procreative attitude" (399). "In no way is it exclusively directed to limiting, much less excluding children; it means also the willingness to accept a larger family" (402).

**9f.** "For just reasons, spouses may wish to space the births of their children. It is their duty to make certain that their desire is not motivated by selfishness but is in conformity with the generosity appropriate to responsible parenthood" (CCC, n. 2368).

**9g.** "As regards the immediate motivation, the encyclical *Humanae Vitae* requires that 'there exist reasonable grounds for spacing births, arising from the physical or psychological condition of husband or wife, or from external circumstances...' (HV 16)" (400). Therefore, the "use of the 'infertile periods' for conjugal union can be an abuse if the couple, for unworthy reasons, seeks in this way to avoid having children, thus lowering the number of births in their family below the morally correct level" (402).

**9h.** "In the common viewpoint it frequently happens that the 'method' [of natural birth regulation is] separated from the ethical dimensions proper to it [and is therefore] put into effect in a merely functional, even utilitarian, way." When this happens "one no longer sees the difference between it and the other 'methods' . . . and one comes to the point of speaking of it as if it were only a different form of contraception" (403).

## 10. The Natural Law

The natural law is often confused with the impersonal "laws of nature" (see CCC, n. 1955).

- The laws of nature pertain to those laws which govern irrational beings.
- "Natural law" pertains to man's rational participation in the divine law.
- John Paul seeks to provide a "personalist"understanding of natural law.
- Natural family planning is acceptable not because it's "not artificial," but because it's in keeping with the nature of man and woman as persons made in God's image.

**10a.** In speaking of the teaching of *Humanae Vitae* as a norm of the natural law, "we mean that 'order of nature' in the field of procreation insofar as it is understood by right reason" (401).

**10b.** Natural law refers to "man not only in the 'natural' aspect of his existence, but also in the integral truth of his personal subjectivity" (397). Thus, the "whole question of . . . *Humanae Vitae* is not reduced simply to the biological dimension of human fertility. . . , but goes back to the very subjectivity of man, to the personal 'I' through which the person is a man or woman" (411).

**10c.** The order of the natural law "is the expression of the Creator's plan for man." Hence, the virtue "expressed in the 'natural' regulation of fertility is determined not so much by fidelity to an impersonal 'natural law' as to the Creator-Person, the source and Lord of the order which is manifested in such a law" (401).

**10d.** "Precisely against the background of [the study we have undertaken] it becomes evident that the . . . moral norm [against contraception] belongs not only to the natural moral law, but also to the *moral order revealed by God.*" Even if it "is not found literally in the Sacred Scripture, nonetheless, . . . this norm is in accordance with the sum total of revealed doctrine, . . . especially [with] biblical anthropology. . . . These are all reasons why every believer and especially every theologian should reread and ever more deeply understand the moral doctrine of the encyclical in this complete context" (389).

**10e.** The Church's teaching is not a matter of "'reducing ethics to biology,' as some have mistakenly held" (402). *Humanae Vitae* stands as a constant reminder that "biological laws . . . involve human personality" (HV, n. 10). Hence, the "naturalness" of "the 'natural method' . . . is 'naturalness' at the level of the person" (414).

## 11. Authentic Conjugal Love

One of the main objections to *Humanae Vitae* is that following its teaching impedes couples from expressing their love for one another. But of what "love" are we speaking — authentic conjugal love that images God, or its perennial counterfeit — concupiscence?

- The teaching of the Church most certainly impedes the expression of concupiscence — *as it should*!
- But it defends and upholds the real possibility of expressing a love which merges the human and the divine (see GS, n. 49). This alone satisfies the desires of the heart.
- Conjugal love is not an "end" of marriage, but its interior principle.

**11a.** In *Humanae Vitae*, Paul VI "wishes to give his teaching on conjugal love an *integral theological meaning*. The whole encyclical is about love [and it] *responds basically to a single question*: what must conjugal love be like in order to discover God's eternal plan of love in it? Under what conditions does conjugal love reflect its prime exemplar, God as Love and God as Father? This is the level upon which we must consider the entire encyclical and the teaching on conjugal love contained therein" (PC, p. 304).

**11b.** Love is "the power given to man in order to participate in that love with which God Himself loves in the mystery of creation and redemption. It is that love which 'rejoices with the truth' (1Co 13:6)." It is that love "in which there is expressed the spiritual joy . . . of every authentic value: a joy like that of the Creator Himself, who in the beginning saw that everything 'was very good' (Gn 1:31)" (406).

**11c.** "The role of love . . . consists...in protecting both the value of the true communion of the spouses and the value of truly responsible fatherhood and motherhood. The power of love . . . is expressed in this, that love *correctly unites 'the two meanings of the conjugal act,'* excluding not only in theory but above all in practice the 'contradiction' that might be evidenced in this field." In reality, "there is no need to speak of 'contradiction' but only of 'difficulty'" (407).

**11d.** "Marriage and conjugal love are by their nature ordered toward the begetting and educating of children" (GS, n. 50). Therefore, a "'true contradiction cannot exist between the divine laws pertaining to the transmission of life and those pertaining to the fostering of authentic conjugal love' (GS, n. 51)" (390).

**11e.** The difficulty of the Church's teaching "arises from the fact that the power of love is implanted in man lured by concupiscence: in human subjects love does battle with . . . the concupiscence of the flesh which distorts the truth of the 'language of the body'" (407).

**11f.** Love "is not able to be realized . . . except through overcoming concupiscence" (407). Concupiscence "makes man in a certain sense blind and insensitive to the most profound values that spring from love and which at the same time constitute love in the interior truth that is proper to it" (409).

**11g.** "If the powers of concupiscence try to detach the 'language of the body' from the truth, . . . the power of love instead strengthens it ever anew in that truth, so that the mystery of the redemption of the body can bear fruit in it. Love itself [is] oriented toward . . . every true good. And therefore its role consists in safeguarding the inseparable connection between the 'two meanings of the conjugal act'" (406).

**11h.** When "the conjugal act [is] deprived of its interior truth, because [it is intentionally] deprived of its procreative capacity, [it] ceases also to be an act of love" (398).

## 12. Self-Mastery, Continence and Chastity

These terms refer to the virtue that makes man *truly free* in his ability to desire and to choose the good in thought and action. Here our previous reflections on "ethic" and "ethos" are decisive.

- One can be "continent" (that is, abstain from sex) for all the wrong reasons.
- Continence *as a virtue* always stems from a desire to uphold the superior *value* of sexual union.
- Only the free man (the one who is master of himself) can love.
- Contraception was not invented to prevent pregnancy! We already had a 100% safe, 100% reliable way of doing that.

**12a.** Continence should not be viewed merely as a temporary "technique." Properly understood, "continence itself is a definite and permanent moral attitude; it is a *virtue*, and therefore, the whole line of conduct guided by it acquires a virtuous character" (400).

**12b.** "The virtuous person tends towards the good with all his sensory and spiritual powers. . . . *Human virtues* . . . order our passions. . . . They make possible ease, self-mastery, and joy in leading a morally good life. The virtuous man is he who freely practices the good" (CCC, n. 1803-1804).

**12c.** The "virtue of continence (self-mastery) . . . is seen to be the fundamental condition for the reciprocal language of the body to remain in the truth and for the couple to 'defer to one another out of reverence for Christ'" (408).

**12d.** "Man is precisely a person because he is master of himself and has self-control. Indeed, insofar as he is master of himself he can 'give himself' to the other. And it is this dimension — the dimension of the liberty of the gift — which becomes essential and decisive for that 'language of the body,' in which man and woman reciprocally express themselves in the conjugal union" (398).

**12e.** "The person [who wants] to succeed in mastering [sexual] impulse and excitement, must be committed to a progressive education in self control of the will, of the feelings, of the emotions; and this education must develop beginning with the most simple acts in which it is relatively easy to put the interior decision into practice" (408).

**12f.** "Self-mastery is a *long and exacting work*. One can never consider it acquired once and for all. It presupposes renewed effort at all stages of life" (CCC, n. 2342).

**12g.** "The conviction that the virtue of continence 'is set against' the concupiscence of the flesh is correct, but it is not altogether complete" (409). "Continence is not only — and not even principally — the ability to 'abstain.' [This] role would be defined as 'negative.' But there is also another role (which we can call 'positive') of self mastery: it is the ability to direct the respective reactions [of emotion and desire], both as to their content and their character" (412).

**12h.** "If conjugal chastity (and chastity in general) is manifested at first as the capacity to resist the concupiscence of the flesh, it later gradually reveals itself as a singular capacity to perceive, love, and practice those meanings of the 'language of the body' which remain altogether unknown to concupiscence itself" (409).

**12i.** "It is often thought that continence causes inner tensions from which man must free himself. In the light of the analyses we have done, continence, understood integrally, is rather the only *way to free man from such tensions*" (411).

**12j.** The "asceticism of continence . . . does not impoverish . . . manifestations [of affection], but rather makes them spiritually more intense and therefore enriches them" (409).

**12k.** "Both the man and the woman, getting away from concupiscence, find the proper dimension of the freedom of the gift [and experience] together the 'language of the body' in a depth, simplicity, and beauty hitherto altogether unknown" (380).

## 13. The "Power" To Love

The Church upholds *Humanae Vitae* with confidence in the "power" of God poured out in the hearts of spouses not only to meet the laws demands, but *ful-fill* them joyfully.

- To whom is this teaching given — to men and women enslaved by weakness and lust, or to men and women set free by the "power" of God to love as He loves?
- To compromise the truth of marital love is to deny the *power* of the Gospel!

**13a.** *Humanae Vitae*'s "view of married life is at every step marked by Christian realism" (405).

**13b.** Through "the sacraments [the Church] flings wide open the channels of grace" (404). "The sacraments inject sanctity into the plan of man's humanity: they penetrate the soul and body, the femininity and masculinity of the personal subject, with the power of sanctity" (378). Sanctity (or holiness) "enables man to express himself deeply with his own body . . . precisely by means of the true 'sincere gift' of himself" (76-77).

**13c.** "'God's love has been poured into our hearts through the Holy Spirit who has been given to us' (Ro 5:5). Here is the essential and fundamental 'power' [to live the truth of *Humanae Vitae*]: *the love planted in the heart . . . by the Holy Spirit*" (405).

**13d.** In becoming "one flesh," spouses "cannot bring about this union on the proper level of persons (*communion personarum*) *except through the powers coming . . . from the Holy Spirit* who purifies, enlivens, strengthens, and perfects the powers of the human spirit" (415).

**13e.** Through prayer and the sacraments "that essential and creative spiritual 'power' of love reaches human hearts and, at the same time, human bodies" (406).

## 14. Respect for the Work of God

This refers to the gift of *piety* which instills an "awe" in us for God and His creation. St. Paul spoke of this when he called spouses to "defer to one another *out of reverence for Christ*" (Eph 5:21).

- Spouses who live with this respect know that they are loved "for their own sakes."
- This respect flows from a spiritually mature/redeemed experience of sexual attraction.

**14a.** In married life, the "attitude of respect for the work of God, which the Spirit stirs up in the couple, has an enormous significance." It leads spouses to "a profound appreciation of the personal dignity of [the other] in their shared life." Such respect gradually frees spouses from "the interior constriction of concupiscence [which is] directed toward the other . . . as an object of pleasure." In turn, it leads to "that 'deep-rooted peace' which is in a certain sense the interior resonance of chastity" (418, 419).

**14b.** The "gift of respect for what comes from God [molds] the couples spirituality to the purpose of protecting the particular dignity of [the conjugal] act." It "leads to understanding among the possible 'manifestations of affection,' the singular, or rather exceptional, significance of [the conjugal] act" (417).

**14c.** The "gift of respect for what is sacred . . . sustains and develops in the married couple a particular *sensitivity to everything* in their vocation and life that bears *the sign of the mystery of creation and redemption*: a sensitivity to everything that is a created reflection of God's wisdom and love." This leads couples to be "filled with veneration for the *essential values of the conjugal union*" (416).

**14d.** "Respect for the work of God contributes to seeing that the conjugal act does not become . . . deprived of the interior meaning of married life as a whole — that it does not become a 'habit.'" It helps to ensure "that there is expressed in [the conjugal act] a sufficient fullness of personal, . . . ethical . . . and . . . religious content." The conjugal act should express "veneration for the majesty of the Creator . . . and for the spousal love of the Redeemer" (418).

## 15. Authentic Marital Spirituality

An authentic marital spirituality leads couples to open their "flesh" — and the "one flesh" they become — to the indwelling power of the Holy Spirit, and thus to be guided by Him in all their life together.

- This Holy Spirit is "the Lord and Giver of Life."
- Every child conceived is a manifestation of the work of the Holy Spirit — a sign of the gift of creation and redemption, a sign of the Holy Spirit's pledge of eternal life.
- Contraception marks a specific "closing off" to the Holy Spirit in conjugal union.
- It marks a "closing off" to participation in the inner life of the Trinity.

**15a.** "In light of . . . *Humanae Vitae*, the fundamental element of the spirituality of married life is the love poured out into the hearts of the couple as a gift of the Holy Spirit (see Ro 5:5). In the sacrament [of marriage] the couple receive this gift along with a special 'consecration'" (415).

**15b.** The "married couple must implore this essential 'power' [of the Holy Spirit] by prayer; . . . they must draw grace and love from the ever-living fountain of the Eucharist; . . . they must overcome 'with humble perseverance' their deficiencies and sins in the Sacrament of Penance. These are the means — *infallible and indispensable* — for forming the Christian spirituality of married life and family life" (406).

**15c.** Education in the theology of the body "already constitutes . . . the essential nucleus of conjugal spirituality" (404).

**15d.** "At the center of the spirituality of marriage . . . lies chastity." Therefore, "*conjugal chastity is also confirmed as 'life by the Spirit'*" (415).

**15e.** "The life 'according to the Spirit' is also expressed in the mutual 'union' . . . whereby the spouses [become] 'one flesh.'" It is "expressed here in the consciousness of the gratification to which there corresponds the dignity of the spouses themselves as [potential] parents." Authentic gratification in conjugal union is naturally integrated with "the profound awareness of the sanctity of the life . . . to which the two [might] give origin, participating — as progenitors — in the forces of the mystery of creation" (349).

**15f.** The "antithesis of conjugal spirituality is constituted, in a certain sense, by the subjective lack of . . . understanding [of the exceptional significance of the conjugal act] which is linked to the contraceptive practice and mentality" (417).

# CONCLUSION
# The Theology of the Body and the New Evangelization

## 1. Antidote to the Culture of Death and Key to the Meaning of Life

If the future of humanity passes by way of marriage and the family (see FC, n. 86), the future of marriage and the family passes by way of the Pope's theology of the body. Herein John Paul provides the "antidote" to the culture of death and a theological foundation for the "new evangelization."

- There will be no renewal of the Church and of the world without a renewal of marriage and the family.
- There will be no renewal of marriage and the family without a return to the full truth of God's plan for the body and sexuality.
- There will be no return to the full truth of God's plan for the body and sexuality without a fresh theological proposal that compellingly demonstrates to the modern world how the Christian sexual ethic — far from the cramped, prudish list of prohibitions it is assumed to be — is a liberating, redeeming ethos that corresponds perfectly with the most noble aspirations of the human heart.
- This is precisely what John Paul II's theology of the body affords. But it also affords so much more!

**1a.** The call to nuptial love and communion inscribed in our masculine and feminine bodies is "the fundamental element of human existence in the world" (16), "the foundation of human life" (EM, 46), and, hence, "the deepest substratum of human ethics and culture"(163).

**1b.** If we live according to the nuptial meaning of the body we "fulfill the very meaning of [our] being and existence" (63).

**1c.** The common life of men and women "constitutes the pure and simple fabric of existence." Thus, "human life, . . . its dignity, its balance, depend, at every moment of history and at every point of geographical longitude and latitude, on 'who' she will be for him and he for her" (159).

**1d.** Confusion about sexual morality "involves a danger perhaps greater than is generally realized: the danger of confusing the basic and fundamental human tendencies, the main paths of human existence. Such confusion must clearly affect the whole spiritual position of man" (LR, p. 66).

**1e.** The "conjugal union . . . is the *natural* foundation, as well as the ontological core, of the family" (PC, p. 339).

**1f.** "It is an illusion to think we can build a true culture of human life if we do not . . . accept and experience sexuality and love and the whole of life according to their true meaning and their close inter-connection" (EV, n. 97).

**1g.** What we learn is obviously "important in regard to marriage and the Christian vocation of husbands and wives." However it "is equally essential and valid for the understanding of man in general: for the fundamental problem of understanding him and for the self-comprehension of his being in the world" (352-353).

**1h.** Even in its limited scope, the Pope's catechesis on the body affords "the rediscovery of the meaning of the whole of existence, the meaning of life" (168). Therefore, "it is this theology of the body which is the basis of the most suitable method of the . . . education (in fact the self-education) of man" (215).

**1i.** "The theology of the body is not merely a theory, but rather a specific, evangelical, Christian pedagogy of the body" (396). "When we speak of the meaning of the body, we refer in the first place to the full awareness of the human being" (124).

**1j.** "John Paul's *Theology of the Body* has ramifications for all of theology. It challenges us to think of sexuality as a way to grasp the essence of the human — and through that, to discern something about the divine. . . . Angelo Scola, rector of the Pontifical Lateran University in Rome, goes so far as to suggest that virtually every thesis in theology — God, Christ, the Trinity, grace, the Church, the sacraments — could be seen in a new light if theologians explored in depth the rich personalism implied in John Paul II's theology of the body. Few contemporary theologians have taken up the challenge implicit in this dramatic proposal. Fewer priests preach these themes. A very small, even microscopic, percentage of the world's Catholics even know that a 'theology of the body' exists" (WH, p. 343).

**1k.** "John Paul's portrait of sexual love as an icon of the interior life of God has barely begun to shape the Church's theology, preaching, and religious education. When it does it will compel a dramatic development of thinking about virtually every major theme in the Creed" (WH, p. 853).

## 2. Reading the "Signs of the Times"

We know not the day nor the hour of Christ's return (see Mt. 24:36).

- Suppose history marches on for another ten thousand years.
- Catholics of the 13th millennium will look at us as members of the "early Church."
- John Paul II will be considered one of the "early" popes.
- Yet his theology of the body will undoubtedly be remembered as a critical moment in the life of that fledgling Church.

We are living in an age that Christians of the future will likely describe as the near-triumph of "the anti-life heresy." They will recount that this heresy threatened to destroy civilization at its roots with its resulting culture of death.

However, as has always been the case in the history of theological development, the Christians of the future will recognize that this attack against God's original plan for human life — commonly referred to in the future as His "marital plan" — will have been vanquished by a precise theological elaboration of the place of the nuptial meaning of the body and the marital covenant at the very heart and center of the economy of salvation (These ideas expressed with gratitude to Sean Inherst).

**2a.** "Andre Malraux was certainly right when he said that the twenty-first century would be the century of religion or it would not be at all" (CTH, p. 229).

**2b.** The world is facing "the greatest historical confrontation humanity has gone through . . . the final confrontation between the Church and the anti-Church, of the Gospel versus the anti-Gospel" (WH, p. 226).

**2c.** "Perhaps we are experiencing the highest level of tension between the Word and the anti-Word in the whole of human history. . . . We may now be wondering if this is the last lap along that way of denial which started out from around the tree of the knowledge of good and evil" (SC, pp. 34-35).

**2d.** "Before Christ's second coming the Church must pass through a final trial that will shake the faith of many believers. The persecution that accompanies her pilgrimage on earth will unveil the 'mystery of iniquity' in the form of a religious deception offering men an apparent solution to their problems at the price of apostasy from the truth" (CCC, n. 675).

**2e.** "We are facing an immense threat to life: not only to the life of individuals but also to that of civilization itself." Despite great scientific and technological progress, we live in "a *society which is sick* and is creating profound distortions in man. Why is this happening? The reason is that our society has broken away from the full truth about man, from the truth about what man and woman really are as persons. Thus it cannot adequately comprehend the real meaning of the gift of persons in marriage, responsible love at the service of fatherhood and motherhood, and the true grandeur of procreation" (LF, nn. 20, 21).

**2f.** The "challenge facing us is an arduous one: only the concerted efforts of all those who believe in the value of life can prevent a setback of unforeseeable consequences for civilization" (EV, n. 91).

**2g.** "If we look at today's world, we are struck by many negative factors that can lead to pessimism. But this feeling is unjustified: we have faith in God our Father and Lord and in his mercy. . . . God is preparing a great springtime for Christianity, and we can already see its first signs" (RM, n. 86)

## 3. What is the New Evangelization?

John Paul first used the expression "the new evangelization" in a pastoral visit to Latin America in 1983. What is "new" is that it is directed not only toward the unbaptized, but towards the modern phenomenon of the "baptized non-believer."

**3a.** The new evangelization is not "a matter of inventing a 'new program.' The program already exists: it is the plan found in the Gospel and in the living Tradition, it is the same as ever" (NMI, n. 29).

**3b.** What is essential in order to meet the unprecedented needs of our day is a proclamation of the Gospel that is "new in ardor, methods, and expression" (John Paul II address March 9, 1983)

**3c.** *Do not empty the cross of its power*! This "is the cry of the new evangelization." For "if the cross of Christ is emptied of its power, man no longer has roots, he no longer has prospects: he is destroyed" (OL, n. 3)!

**3d.** The "*new evangelization* [involves] a vital effort to come to a deeper understanding of the mysteries of faith and to find meaningful language with which to convince our contemporaries that they are called to newness of life through God's love." It is the task of sharing with modern men and women "the 'unsearchable riches of Christ' and of making known 'the plan of the mystery hidden for ages in God who created all things' (Eph 3:8-9)" (SE, pp. 53, 55).

## 4. The Theology of the Body Incarnates the Gospel

John Paul's catechesis demonstrates that the Gospel is not "out there" somewhere. It is not abstract. An image of God's mystery is stamped right in us — in our deepest spiritual longings for intimacy and communion and in our very bodies as male and female.

- We can preach that "Jesus is the *answer*" until we're blue in the face. But unless people are in touch with the *question* this remains an abstraction.
- By grounding the Gospel in the human experience of embodiment, the theology of the body is the antidote to theological abstraction.
- The universal human question is the experience and "ache" of solitude.
- The divine answer given to the universal human question is communion.
- If the Gospel is not "incarnated" with essentially human experiences, it is essentially not the Gospel of Jesus Christ.
- The new evangelization is not first an appeal to abstract principles, but to the desires of the human heart for love and communion — and the compelling witness that Jesus is the answer to that longing for communion.
- Christ fully reveals man to himself and makes his supreme calling (communion) clear!

**4a.** "God comes to us in the things we know best and can verify most easily, the things of our everyday life, apart from which we cannot understand ourselves" (FR, n. 12).

**4b.** The Church "in her whole being and in all her members . . . is sent to announce, bear witness, make present, and spread the mystery of the communion of the Holy Trinity" (CCC, n. 738).

**4c.** "To make the Church *the home and school of communion*: that is the great challenge facing us in the millennium which is now beginning, if we wish to be faithful to God's plan and respond to the world's deepest yearnings" (NMI, n. 43).

**4d.** "We need to bring the *Gospel of life* to the heart of every man and woman and to make it penetrate every part of society. This involves above all proclaiming *the core* of this Gospel. It is the proclamation of a living God who is close to us, who calls us to profound communion with himself and awakens in us the certain hope of eternal life. It is the affirmation of the inseparable connection between the person, his life and his bodiliness. It is the presentation of human life as a life of relationship, a gift of God, the fruit and sign of his love. It is the proclamation that Jesus has a unique relationship with every person, which enables us to see in every human face the face of Christ. It is the call for a 'sincere gift of self' as the fullest way to realize our personal freedom. [As a consequence] the meaning of life is found in giving and receiving love, and in this light human sexuality and procreation reach their true and full significance" (EV, n. 81).

**4e.** Understanding Christ's revelation regarding the human body and its redemption "concerns the entire Bible" (249). It plunges us into "the perspective of the whole Gospel, of the whole teaching, in fact, of the whole mission of Christ" (175).

## 5. The Church's Response to Modern Rationalism

Descartes' dictum, "I think therefore I am," marks the shift that inaugurated modern rationalism.

- Man becomes a "mind" divorced from his body.
- Reality is reduced to what I can "figure out" — mystery is not tolerated.
- Subjective thoughts are no longer answerable to objective reality.

- This marks the "great divorce" of man from the "nuptial mystery."

**5a.** "Saint Paul's magnificent synthesis concerning the 'great mystery' appears as the compendium or *summa*, in some sense, *of the teaching about God and man* which was brought to fulfillment by Christ. Unfortunately, Western thought, with the development of *modern rationalism*, has been gradually moving away from this teaching. The philosopher who formulated the principle . . . 'I think, therefore I am,' also gave the modern concept of man its distinctive dualistic character. It is typical of rationalism to make a radical contrast in man between spirit and body, between body and spirit. The body can never be reduced to mere matter: it is a *spiritualized body*, just as man's spirit is so closely united to the body that he can be described as *an embodied spirit*. The richest source for knowledge of the body is the Word made flesh. *Christ reveals man to himself.* In a certain sense, this statement of the Second Vatican Council is the reply, so long awaited, which the Church has given to modern rationalism" (LF, n. 19).

**5b.** "Modern rationalism *does not tolerate mystery*. It does not accept the mystery of man as male and female, nor is it willing to admit that the full truth about man has been revealed in Jesus Christ. In particular, it does not accept the 'great mystery' proclaimed in the *Letter to the Ephesians* but radically opposes it. It may well acknowledge, in the context of a vague deism, the possibility, or even the need for a supreme or divine Being. But it firmly rejects the idea of a God who become man in order to save man. For rationalism, it is unthinkable that God should be the Redeemer, much less that *he should be 'the bridegroom,'* the primordial and unique source of the human love between spouses. Rationalism provides a radically different way of looking at creation and the meaning of human existence. But once man begins to lose sight of a God who loves him, a God who calls man through Christ to live in him and with him, and once the family no longer has the possibility of sharing in the 'great mystery,' what is left except the mere *temporal dimension of life*? Earthly life becomes nothing more than the scenario of a battle for existence, a desperate search for gain, and financial gain before all else. The deep-seated roots of the 'great mystery,' the sacrament of life and love which began with Creation and Redemption and *which has Christ the Bridegroom as its ultimate surety*, have been lost in the modern way of looking at things. The 'great mystery' is threatened in us and all around us" (LF, n. 19).

Insert *Gaudium et Spes* 22 into the equation and it unmasks the sham of modern rationalism: "The religion of the God who became man," said Paul VI in his closing speech at the Council, encounters "the religion (for such it is) of man who makes himself God" (Cited in *Closing Speeches: Vatican Council II* [Daughters of St. Paul], p. 10)

- To you who, with Descartes, would say "I think, therefore I am," turn to Him who says "I am because I am" (see Jn 8:58).
- To you who have lost the meaning of birth, life, suffering, and death, turn to Him who was born, lived, suffered, died — and rose again!
- To you who think life is a battle to gain more and more, sell all you have and give the money to the poor (see Mt 19:21).
- To you who think freedom comes from rejecting any claim to truth, turn to Him who is the Truth and He will set you free.
- To you who do not know love, turn to Him who is love and receive the gift He gives — His own divine life.
- Abandon yourself entirely to Him. Live as He lives, love as He loves and you will find yourself.

## 6. Crossing the Threshold of Hope

Many of us are like the disciples on the road to Emmaus — baffled by the tragic events of our own day, wondering what it all means and why it has all gone so sour.

- The Vicar of Christ has walked with us, opening up the Scriptures for us.
- "Were not our hearts burning within us as he unfolded the 'great mystery' of God's designs" (see Lk 24:32)?
- And just as the disciples came to recognize Christ "in the breaking of the bread" — in His body given for them in Eucharist — so, too, have we come to see Christ revealed in His body: in our bodies because we, though many, are "one body" with Him.

At the beginning of the third Christian millennium, it is time for the Church and the world to "cross the threshold of hope" into a new springtime. It is time to make our "passover" from a culture of death to a culture of life.

**6a.** "We are certainly not seduced by the naive expectation that, faced with the great challenges of our time, we shall find some magic formula. No, we shall not be saved by a formula, but by a Person, and the assurance which he gives us: *I am with you*!" (NMI, n. 29). Christ the Bridegroom is with us (see LF, part II)!

**6b.** With the celebration of the Great Jubilee "a new time of advent" is upon us, "at the end of which, like two thousand years ago, 'every man will see the salvation of God.'" In journeying to that end, a collision between the forces of good and evil "may in many cases be of a tragic nature and may perhaps lead to fresh defeats for humanity" (DV, n. 56).

**6c.** Man and woman's call to life-giving communion "is placed at the center of the great struggle between good and evil, between life and death, between love and all that is opposed to love" (LF, n. 23).

**6d.** But in the midst of this great clash "the Church firmly believes that on God's part there is always a salvific self-giving" (DV, n. 56). "Who will win? The one who welcomes the gift" (DV, n. 55).

*Mary, Mother of God . . .*

*Mary, bride without spot or wrinkle or any such thing . . .*

*Mary, one who welcomes the gift . . .*

*Pray for us that we might welcome the gift,*

*now and at the hour of our death. Amen.*

# Suggested Reading

Albacete, Lorenzo. *God at the Ritz: Attraction to Infinity* (New York: The Crossroad Publishing Co., 2002) — An exploration of man's continuing fascination with the eternal mysteries even in the midst of a skeptical, materialistic culture, with John Paul II's theology of the body and vision of the human person as a constant backdrop.

Asci, Donald. *The Conjugal Act as a Personal Act: A Study of the Catholic Concept of the Conjugal Act in the Light of Christian Anthropology* (San Francisco: Ignatius Press, 2002) — Places John Paul II's theology of the body in the context of Catholic thinking on the conjugal act and the human person, with ample commentary on John Paul II's contribution.

Beigel, Gerard. *Faith and Social Justice in the Teaching of Pope John Paul II* (Washington D.C.: Peter Lang Publishing Inc., 1997) — An analysis of how John Paul II's anthropology informs the social teachings of the Church.

Hogan, Richard M. and John M. Levoir. *Covenant of Love*, 2d ed. (San Francisco: Ignatius Press, 1992) — The first book to summarize portions of John Paul II's theology of the body for a general audience, including a commentary on the 1981 apostolic exhortation *Familiaris Consortio*.

John Paul II. *The Theology of the Body: Human Love in the Divine Plan* (Boston: Pauline Books and Media, 1997) — The entire 129 Wednesday general audience lectures that comprise John Paul II's theology of the body under one cover, with an appendix including *Humanae Vitae*, *Mulieris Dignitatum*, and *Evangelium Vitae*.

Little, Joyce. *The Church and the Culture War: Secular Anarchy or Sacred Order?* (San Fransisco: Ignatius Press, 1995) — A deconstruction of secular society and its many ills particularly radical feminism based on John Paul II's theology of the body.

Schmitz, Kenneth L. *At the Center of the Human Drama: The Philosophical Anthropology of Karol Wojtyla / John Paul II* (Washington, D.C.: Catholic University of America Pres, 1993) — Demonstrates how John Paul II links the valid insights of modern philosophy to the traditional metaphysics of the great philosophers of the middle ages.

Shivanandan, Mary. *Crossing the Threshold of Love: A New Vision of Marriage in the Light of John Paul II's Anthropology* (Washington, D.C.: Catholic University of America Press, 1999) — An in-depth analysis of the evolution of John Paul II's anthropology and how it has transformed our understanding of the meaning of marriage and human sexuality.

Schu, Rev. Walter, LC, *The Splendor of Love: John Paul II's Vision of Marriage and Family* (New Hope, KY: Catholics United for Life, 2002) — A summary of John Paul II's extensive teaching on sexuality, marriage, and family life, including a section devoted to the Pope's theology of the body.

Von Hildebrand, Dietrich. *Marriage: The Mystery of Faithful Love* (Manchester, NH: Sophia Institute Press, 1991) — Originally published in 1929, one of the earliest "personalist" analyses of marriage, helps to put the work of John Paul II in philosophical and historical context.

West, Christopher. *Good News about Sex and Marriage: Answers to Your Honest Questions about Catholic Teaching* (Ann Arbor, MI: Servant Publications, 2000) — The presenter of this seminar series uses John Paul II's insights to answer the toughest questions and objections to Church teaching on sex and marriage, demonstrating that teaching corresponds to the deepest desires of the heart.

West, Christopher. *Theology of the Body Explained: A Commentary on John Paul II's "Gospel of the Body"* (Boston, MA: Pauline Books & Media, 2003) — The first book available to explain systematically the entirety of the Pope's catechesis on the body.

Wojtyla, Karol. *Love and Responsibility* (San Francisco: Ignatius Press, 1993)—Originally published in 1960, future Pope John Paul II lays down the philosophical foundations for the theology of the body, drawing on his extensive pastoral work with engaged and married couples.

NOTES

# Guidelines for Group Study

Since the first edition of this series, numerous study groups have started around the country. This is a wonderful way to discover and share the enlightening, inspiring revelations in Pope John Paul II's theology of the body. You could:

- Organize a group through your local church, advertising your meetings in the church bulletin or during announcements at the end of the Sunday liturgy.
- Invite friends to gather in your home to listen to the series together over the course of several weekly meetings. (A group of 2-5 married or engaged couples would be especially fitting.)
- Listen to the series with your spouse or fiance(e). John Paul II's vision of marriage can have a powerful influence on a couple who are open to loving each other more perfectly.
- Contact the organizations below to network with other study groups around the country and get ideas for your group:

Theology of the Body Evangelization Team (TOBET)
972-849-6543 / info@tobet.org
The Love and Responsibility Foundation
917-846-3798 / info@catholicculture.com

Whether studying *A Crash Course in the Theology of the Body* with a large group or as a couple, the following guidelines should help make the experience productive and satisfying. Additional copies of this study guide are available so each participant can have a copy (see About This Study Guide, page iii).

1. *Opening prayer* — As series presenter Christopher West makes clear, prayer must be our foundation as we seek to understand, appreciate and be tranformed by John Paul II's theology of the body. Opening each group study session with a prayer is essential.

2. *Reflections on previous lectures* — Pope John Paul II's vision in the theology of the body so radically challenges our preconceptions and assumptions about the body and sex that many of his ideas will sink in only gradually. Allow some time at the start of each session for discussion of any insights or questions encountered while reflecting on the lectures covered so far.

3. *Listening to the lecture* — Follow along with the lecture in your study guides. Feel free to pause or rewind the lecture from time to time if anyone misses a key point. Anyone who has studied the series before might briefly offer insight on any unclear points as you go. You may want to devote more than one meeting to longer lectures. In fact, you may wish to spread each lecture out over 2-4 meetings, depending on length.

4. *Discussion and questions on the lecture* — Though you do not have the opportunity to ask questions directly to Christopher West, you can deepen your understanding of the lecture you just heard by sharing your questions and reflections together. Reviewing the key concepts in each lecture should be helpful as well.

5. *Closing prayer* — Closing each session with a prayer will prepare your heart and mind to embrace more fully the theology of the body before your next meeting, and beyond.

## Additional Quotes

1. [Speaking of marriage and the family] "In this entire world there is not a more perfect, more complete image of God, Unity and Community. There is no other human reality which corresponds more, humanly speaking, to that divine mystery" (JP II, homily Dec 30, 1988).

2. The "giving and the accepting of the gift interpenetrate, so that the giving itself becomes accepting, and the accepting is transformed into giving" (TB, 71).

3. There is a "bond that exists between the dignity of the human being (man or woman) and the nuptial meaning of his body." The more we experience the redemption of the body the more we "discover and strengthen that bond" (TB, 301).

4. Christ's words in the Sermon on the Mount are "an invitation to a pure way of looking at others, capable of respecting the spousal meaning of the body" (VS, n. 15).

5. Purity of heart manifests "a tranquil testimony of conscience" because it "preserves an interior faithfulness to the gift according to the nuptial meaning of the body" (TB, 69).

6. "We cannot acquire ...purity without renunciation, without inner struggles against our own weakness; but once acquired, this maturity of heart and mind makes up a hundred-fold for the efforts it rewards. The result is a new spontaneity of feeling, of gesture and of behavior that facilitates relations with [other] people, especially with children" (JP II, Be Not Afraid, p. 16).

7. "Man understands his liberty according to whether [or not] he is free" (JP II, Be Not Afraid, p. 97).

8. If with Christ you died to the principles of this world, why do you live as if you still belonged to the world? Why do you submit to human regulations such as, "Do not handle, Do not taste, Do not touch"? These indeed have an appearance of wisdom in promoting rigor and devotion and severity to the body, but they are of no value in checking the indulgence of the flesh (see Col 2:20-23).

9. Acquiring true freedom "is a still an uncertain and fragile journey as long as we are on earth, but it is one made possible by grace, which enables us to possess the full freedom of the children of God (see Rom 8:21)" (VS, n. 18).

10. As soon as you entered [the font], then, you divested yourself of your garment; this gesture symbolized the divesting yourself of the old man in you with all his practices. Disrobed, you were naked, symbolizing in this Christ who was nailed naked to the Cross, and by his very nudity defeated the principalities and powers, dragging them into his triumphal cortege... O marvelous thing, you were naked before everyone and yet you did not blush for shame. Truly you represented in this the image of the first man, Adam, who in paradise was naked but was not ashamed (St. Cyril of Jerusalem, Mystagogical Catecheses 2:2).

11. Celibacy for the kingdom "makes evident, even in the renunciation of marriage, the 'nuptial meaning' of the body through ...a personal gift to Jesus Christ and his Church which prefigures and anticipates the perfect and final communion and self-giving of the world to come.... [It prefigures] also in a bodily way, the eschatological marriage of Christ with the Church" (JP II, Pastores Dabo Vobis, n. 29).

12. In the Latin Church, priests "are normally chosen from among men of faith who live a celibate life and who intend to remain celibate 'for the sake of the kingdom of heaven'" (CCC, n. 1579).

13. "We believe in something preternatural that has come into the world for the very purpose of disturbing and stifling the fruits of the Second Vatican Council, and to prevent the Church from bursting into a hymn of joy at having regained full awareness of herself" (Paul VI, Feast of Sts. Peter & Paul, 1978).

14. "The defense of human life must begin at the very source of human existence. ...We did no more than accept this charge when, 10 years ago, we published the encyclical Humanae Vitae. ... We have made these statements motivated only by our supreme responsibilities as universal teacher and pastor, and for the good of humanity" (Paul VI, Feast of Sts. Peter & Paul, 1978).